In My Name

They Shall Lay Hands on the Sick, and They Shall Recover

Millie McIlvaine

Printed in the United States of America

ISBN: 0692931236
ISBN 13: 9780692931233

Scriptures marked KJV are taken from the King James Version (KJV): King James Version, public domain.

Scriptures marked (AMPCE) are taken from the Amplified Bible Classic Edition. Copyright © 1954, 1958, 1962, 1964, 1965, 1987 by The Lockman Foundation. Used by permission. (www.lockman.org)

Scriptures marked (AMP) are taken from the Amplified Bible. Copyright © 1954, 1958, 1962, 1964, 1965, 1987 by the Lockman Foundation. Used by permission. (www.lockman.org)

Scriptures marked (NKJV) are taken from the New King James Version®. Copyright © 1982 by Thomas Nelson. Used by permission. All rights reserved.

The cover artwork is by Justine Peterson. Justine is a watercolorist and mixed media artist who creates spiritual portrait and figurative work. "And Now I See" illustrates the moment Christ healed a blind man. The conceptualization behind it was to capture the very moment and emotion when the man's eyes were opened and he saw his Savior. Justine and her husband Rod own Gethsemane Fine Art, a print company for their works of art. Together they hope to spread their testimonies of Christ and His love. They currently reside in Southern Utah with their three children. (www.gethsemanefineart.com)

Book title, *In My Name*, Mark 16:17-18 (KJV): King James Version, public domain.

Dedication

This book is dedicated to Jesus, my Lord and Savior. Thank You, Holy Spirit, for leading me, teaching me, and for Your faithfulness, mercy, grace, and great love. To my wonderful husband, Jim, who loves me unconditionally and encourages me every day. To my beautiful daughter, Kim, and my amazing grandson, Jacob, who make our lives full and rewarding. To my parents for their love, support, and sacrifices. To my accomplished brother, Tony. To my brother, Sam, you left us far too soon. I miss you, and because of your profession of faith in Jesus, I know you see Him, face-to-face. To our pastor, Joseph Zaino, for guiding, encouraging, and praying for us through this writing process. To Kathy Curtis for copyediting and interior design (www.christianbookformat.com).

Table of Contents

Introduction

My book is a prophetic compilation of times spent in the presence of the Holy Spirit, listening and studying the Word of God. It is inspired by the Holy Spirit for the purpose of teaching and training others to heal the sick. The message is His; the desire to heal is His. It comes from His heart with His love, for His creation. Do you need a healing miracle or know someone who does?

I've spent thirty-seven years praying for and healing the sick. There's never been a disease impossible for God. Each chapter of my book is arranged by the leading of the Holy Spirit to build your faith. Healing is neither a formula nor empty, rote words. It doesn't come by hoping, but by your faith in the Word of God. I teach scriptural truths and show you how to access what Jesus has already provided in the atonement of Calvary's cross. Your healing was supplied when Jesus was scourged. His stripes have already healed you. Healing is waiting for you to receive it.

The Holy Spirit isn't healing anyone today. Rather, He is manifesting Himself in signs and wonders, miracles, and healings, which have already been provided by Jesus. I show you how, by faith, to receive what's in the spiritual realm and bring it to the physical realm. Walking in the supernatural requires faith and knowledge. The reader who applies these truths and launches out into the deep will be the one who sees the greatest miracles.

If you need healing or you desire to be used as a vessel of healing by the Holy Spirit, my book teaches you how to be successful. All healing is a manifestation of the Holy Spirit. His gifts flow through prepared vessels. As you read and study, the Holy Spirit will teach you. My book equips the Body of Christ, strengthens faith, and gives the keys to legal authority and dominion in Christ. You will receive fresh revelation backed up by Scripture and teaching, demonstrating the Word of God for today's move of God.

Now is the hour of great miracles and the outpouring of God's power. Large healing crusades are stepping aside as God raises up individuals and teaches them how to access His power and authority. God's grace will usher in the next global revival, the likes of which have never been seen before. Signs and wonders will convince unbelievers and believers that Jesus is who He says He is. Like small campfires dotting the night landscape, the Holy Spirit is birthing revival flames, which will catch and ignite in those who carry Jesus Christ within their earthen vessels. This coming revival will spring forth across nations. God will send a tsunami of grace for the lost and the dying by raising up those who will release His power and flow in His Spirit. God wants to use you.

There are additional Scripture and discussion opportunities at the end of each chapter. This book is an excellent teaching tool for Sunday school classes, Bible study, and home fellowship groups for all ages from teen to adult.

Come As You Are

I would like to give you an invitation to receive Jesus as your personal Lord and Savior. If you have never asked God to forgive you, you can do that now. You can have a relationship with God through His Son, Jesus. Perhaps you've gone to church for a long time and been faithful to your denomination, but you've never been born again. Maybe you've heard the term "born again" but don't understand it. You aren't sure if you're born again, and you want to make sure.

Possibly you've acknowledged Jesus as Lord of your life and you want to take the next step in your walk with Him. You might also be someone who once had a relationship with Jesus, but it has grown cold. Things in your life have taken the place of your love and affection for God and you would like to rededicate yourself to Him, making Him first again. Jesus loves you and extends an invitation for all to come back to Him. He does not condemn you. Whatever your situation, if you want to see the Kingdom of God, Jesus said that you must be born again.

Simply stated, all have sinned, and no one has lived a pure, holy life. Everyone is born into sin, which has the penalty of death. Baptism does not remove sin; only the blood of Jesus takes away sin. Because of sin, you're separated from God and spiritually dead. The good news of the Gospel is this: Jesus came to bring you salvation and eternal life. God loves you and there is life after death. You will enter heaven or hell.

Heaven is God's home. A place where there is no more suffering or sorrow. A place of indescribable beauty and joy. Hell is a place of horror and torment prepared for Satan and his demons. It is unimaginable darkness and anguish. A place of devouring fear and evil. Hell has no comfort or provision.

God does not want anyone to go to hell, so He sent His only begotten Son to prevent eternal damnation. The only way a person goes to hell is to reject Jesus and to deny His existence. In the same way, a person goes to heaven by asking God to forgive their sins and receiving Jesus as their Savior. There is no other way to the Father and to heaven except through His Son, Jesus.

Jesus came to this earth two thousand years ago to take your punishment and die in your place. In exchange He offers you a new life, not born in the flesh, but born in the spirit. No one can save themselves; no one can pay the debt of their sins. No one can live good enough to stand in the presence of Almighty God. God ordained that the only payment for your sins was the shedding of His blood.

He came down from heaven and took on human form. He was crucified on the cross for the sins of the world. To go to heaven, you must acknowledge what Jesus did, ask for forgiveness, and receive Him as your personal Lord and Savior. If you will pray this prayer and mean it in your heart, Jesus will save you. He will give you His Holy Spirit to teach you and take you to heaven when you die. Don't put this off; tomorrow is not promised to you. Today is your day for salvation. Bow your head and repeat this prayer:

> *Dear Lord Jesus, I am a sinner and I cannot save myself from death. I believe You came and died on the cross for me, taking my sins and giving me Your life. I want to be born again and live with You forever. I ask You to forgive all my sins and to cleanse me in Your blood. I renounce darkness and the works of the devil in my life. I ask You into my heart, to come and make Your home in me. Save me and forgive me. Please be my Lord and Savior. Teach me Your ways and guide me. Give me Your life and make me new and clean and born again. Come, Lord Jesus. I open the door to You. You are welcome in my life. Thank You, Jesus. Amen.*

If you confess with your mouth that Jesus is Lord and you believe in your heart He was resurrected from the dead, you are saved. If you invite Him into your life and trust Him, you are born again. Eternal life begins the moment you receive Jesus as your Lord and Savior. To walk in the anointing, to fellowship with God, and to receive forgiveness for your sins, you must come the way God ordains. There is only one way to God and eternal life. It is to trust Jesus to be your Lord and Savior.

Some evidence of your new birth will be a deep sense of peace and faith in knowing Jesus is real. You will have a desire to be close to Him and to know the Bible. You'll understand what's right and what's wrong, and you'll want to choose to be good, to love God, and not sin. Your life will take on new meaning. You'll know God really loves you and is living within you. Old, sinful things you used to do will no longer be pleasing to you. Open your Bible daily and learn Scripture. The Holy Spirit will help you and teach you what the Bible means. Get into a good Bible-believing church and attend often. Be baptized in water and in the Holy Spirit. You cannot grow in Christ without the help of strong Christians and God's Word. God loves you so much He died for you. Will you live for Him?

Today I decided to accept Jesus as my Lord and Savior.
Today's date: _____.
I believe in Romans 10:8-13 for my salvation.

If you need prayer for healing, please contact me. If you decided to trust Jesus as your Lord and Savior, I would like to hear from you. You may contact me via email. If your need is urgent, please put "URGENT" in your subject line. Email address: Milliemcilvaine@ yahoo.com

Baptism of the Holy Spirit

The Holy Spirit is the third person of the Godhead Trinity. He is the One sent by the Father to the New Testament Church. He resides within born-again believers to guide them and to empower and immerse the Body of Christ into the life of the Spirit. After salvation and water baptism, the baptism in the Holy Spirit is the next step in our Christian faith. Many people stop at water baptism, but there is another baptism. John foretold of it when he said one would come after him and would baptize in the Spirit. Jesus baptized His disciples on Pentecost with the Holy Spirit, giving them the power to be His witnesses and to preach the Gospel. This baptism immerses us into the same power and life as that of the apostles. If you've never received the baptism of the Holy Spirit, this chapter will explain in more detail and lead you in prayer.

CHAPTER 1

Baptism of the Holy Spirit

When Jesus was on earth, He revealed Himself and His heavenly Father. He explained that He and His Father were in perfect union. Because of Jesus's teachings, we are able to form a vision of both Him and His Father. As Jesus's time on earth was ending, He promised His disciples to send someone to take His place. He described this person as the one who would help them, teach them, lead them, strengthen them, and encourage them. Part of the mystery of the Holy Spirit is due to His anonymity. He doesn't draw attention to Himself. He makes Jesus known to the world, testifies of Him, and teaches the believer about Him. One morning in my quiet time with God, I asked the Holy Spirit to tell me more about Himself. These are the words He spoke to my spirit:

I am the Voice and the Power to the Church of Jesus Christ in this hour. I am Wisdom made manifest; I am always in operation. Oil and wind and fire and rain are used to describe Me. Flowing, rushing, and moving describe My powerful energy. I give gifts and impartation, direction, and guidance to the Church. I orchestrate the Body of Christ to be in perfect harmony with the Head, who is Jesus Christ. My work is to glorify Him. He is the Head, above all things seen and unseen. I speak within you and give you power, instruction, and wisdom. I am sent to reveal truth, light, righteousness, justice, mercy, and forgiveness. I convict while not condemning.

My residence within you is your peace and joy. I teach you and give you revelation. I reveal hidden things both natural and supernatural. I am your constant companion; I never leave you unattended. I open the Word to your understanding and teach you about the Kingdom of God. I do not draw attention to Myself, for I do not promote Myself. I work to turn your face to the Father, to have you behold His goodness and love. I am the Spirit of Jesus.

Just as you have an inner spirit, I am that very Spirit, I live in your spirit. To know Me better is to live and walk not in the flesh but in the Spirit. You will not find me in the flesh or in the mind. I occupy your spirit man. Walking with me in the Spirit is true living, true life. It is eternal life that never ages, never dies, never dries up, and never runs out. It is continual, flowing, and moving, like a river.

I am peace, contentment, and joy. I never speak on My own behalf but rather speak at the direction of God, the Father. We are in perfect union and perfect harmony. We uphold the Kingdom of God. I deliver to you the Kingdom life. I reveal Scripture to you, and I bring the light of Christ across your pathway. I sow light and revelation before you. I give instruction and wisdom in all matters of the Church and to individuals. I am the Voice of the Church in this present hour. I edify believers. I convict, teach, and train you so that you can be successful in overcoming this world and all the lusts of the flesh in this worldly chaos.

Who Is the Holy Spirit?

The Holy Spirit is the third person of the Trinity. He appears eight times from Genesis to Malachi and is referred to as the Spirit of God. However, from Matthew to Revelation, He appears 157 times and is referred to as the Holy Spirit or Holy Ghost. Jesus came into this world to destroy the works of the devil, to show us the Father, and bring salvation to all who would believe in Him. Before going to the cross, Jesus promised to send His followers another Helper. Fifty days after His resurrection, on the Jewish Feast of Weeks or Pentecost, Jesus ushered in the Holy Spirit.[1] The Feast of Weeks or Pentecost means the number fifty because it falls fifty days after the Feast of First Fruits, and First Fruits falls three days after the Feasts of Unleavened Bread and Passover. Why is this important?

When God gave Moses the law, He commanded seven holy feasts to be observed.[2] Four were known as spring feasts and three as fall feasts. Jesus fulfilled the spring feasts during His time here on earth. He became our Passover Lamb on Calvary and our sinless Unleavened Bread at His hour of death. He rose from the dead three days after His crucifixion and became the First Fruits offering to God in resurrection new life.

Forty days after His resurrection, Jesus ascended into heaven to sit at the Father's right hand. Ten days later, which is fifty days (Pentecost) after the Feast of First Fruits, He introduced the Holy Spirit. The three remaining fall feasts must also be fulfilled by Jesus and will happen at His second coming. They are the Feasts of Trumpets, which is Rosh Hashanah. This signals the rapture of the Church by the blowing of the trumpet. The Day of Atonement, which is Yom Kippur, is the time when the Jews will behold Jesus as

---

[1] *Got Questions?org,* "What is the Feast of Weeks?" https://www.gotquestions.org/Feast-of-Weeks.html.
[2] *Got Questions?org,* "What are the different Jewish festivals in the Bible?" *https://www.gotquestions.org/Jewish-festivals.html.*

Messiah and repent of their sin of rejecting Him. The final feast is Tabernacles or Sukkot. This is when Jesus sets up His millennial reign in Jerusalem and lives with us.

On the Feast of Pentecost, the Holy Spirit came with a mighty public demonstration of power to the 120 in the Upper Room at Jerusalem. In a spectacular array of manifestation and authority, He appeared as tongues of fire over each of their heads. They began to speak in new tongues, new languages, and to prophesy. On that day three thousand people were saved, and the New Testament Church was birthed. This was the Holy Spirit's entrance to usher in and lead the Church. The Holy Spirit was before creation, before any form, when the earth was empty darkness. Together with the Father and the Son, they created the heavens and the earth, making light, forming man and all things created.

I believe we don't enjoy fellowshipping with the Holy Spirit because we don't acknowledge Him. The Holy Spirit is God in power, in grace, and in beauty. He is the Spirit of Jesus. He is Truth. He is wisdom made manifest. He is the Teacher. He is the Helper and the sweetness of God's mercy to those who have placed their faith and trust in Jesus as Lord and Savior. He speaks in perfect oneness with the Father, testifying of the Son.

The Kingdom of God is here, with all authority and power, living inside each born-again believer. Those who submit to His leading will live a life in the Spirit. They will walk in God's will because the Holy Spirit discerns the will of the Father for each member of the Body of Christ and brings it to fruition. They will flow in the gifts of the Holy Spirit, demonstrating the power and love of God to the world.

The moment you were born again you were sealed with the Holy Spirit. Marked as God's dear child, you are protected to the time of Jesus's return. He will never leave you nor forsake you. If you have never developed a personal relationship with the Holy Spirit, I encourage you to begin. He will respond to you, open Scriptures for your understanding, give you gifts, and use you in the Kingdom of God here on earth. He brings peace and joy, bearing in us the fruit of righteousness.

He unlocks the mysteries of the Bible and makes God's love and mercy evident to believers. He's the voice of the Church in this hour, leading and orchestrating the Body of Christ worldwide. He speaks and confirms truth that Jesus is Messiah. He will not intrude or push His way on you. He comes by invitation and teaches all things. He leads you in pure worship to God, worship in Spirit and in Truth.

The Holy Spirit demonstrated Himself before and during the life of Jesus here on earth. He caused John the Baptist to leap in his mother's womb when Mary visited Elizabeth. He impregnated Mary with Jesus even though she was a virgin. He spoke through dreams and angels to guide Joseph and Mary to Egypt away from King Herod. He opened the mind of John and led him to prepare the way for Jesus's ministry by baptizing in water.

John foretold Jesus would come and baptize them with the Holy Spirit. At the baptism of Jesus in the Jordan River, He manifested as a dove, signifying His abiding presence on Jesus and God's approval.

Only those who have been born again can receive the Holy Spirit. The world has no knowledge of Him, yet He is in full operation to convict, in hopes all would repent and come to Jesus. He is our Comforter in times of trials and sorrow. He is the truth when deception ensnares us. He is our Teacher, opening up the Word of God by giving us revelations. He brings Scripture to mind when we need it. He is our Intercessor through Jesus to the Father. He is more than a conscience when we sin. He is our conviction and our repentance to righteousness in Christ. He not only hears our prayers, but He also moves on our behalf to answer.

> **John 16:8-11 (KJV)**
> **⁸ And when he is come, he will reprove the world of sin, and of righteousness, and of judgment: ⁹ of sin, because they believe not on me; ¹⁰ of righteousness, because I go to my Father, and ye see me no more; ¹¹ of judgment, because the prince of this world is judged.**

This passage of Scripture explains three distinct purposes of the Holy Spirit's work in the world today. First, He convicts the entire world of sin, a conviction which either leads to repentance or a seared conscience towards sin and rejection of Christ and of salvation. Second, the Holy Spirit works to convince us we are not righteous by our own good works. The only righteousness God accepts is the righteousness of His Son. This is a foundational truth for every believer.

Christ is our righteousness. Through His shed blood and our faith in Him, we're made in right standing with God. It's not our good works that justify us; it's our faith in Jesus that justifies us. No amount of good works can get a person saved and into heaven. Finally, the Holy Spirit brings judgment against Satan because Jesus defeated him. The Holy Spirit reveals the believer's authority over Satan. The devil was judged by Christ's sacrifice on the cross. Just as Jesus told His disciples they needed the baptism of the Holy Spirit, so too we need this baptism. We are ineffective apart from the gifts of the Spirit. Healing and miracles are two of the gifts of the Holy Spirit. We can't operate in His gifts until we are baptized in Him.

What Is the Baptism of the Holy Spirit?

The baptism of the Holy Spirit is a separate experience from salvation and water baptism. In this baptism we are not immersed in water; we are immersed in the Spirit's life and power. The Holy Spirit's baptism empowers the believer to serve in the Kingdom of God.

Once a person professes Jesus as his personal Lord and Savior, he, like the disciples, is commanded to go into all the world and preach this Gospel until Jesus returns.

The early church disciples needed the power of the Holy Spirit to preach, teach, heal the sick, raise the dead, and cast out demons. How much more do we need the power of the Holy Spirit to do the same today? It is God, the Father, who introduces us to God, the Son. It is the Son (Jesus) who introduces us to the Holy Spirit. Man baptizes with water. Jesus is the baptizer in the Holy Spirit.

Why Do We Need the Baptism of the Holy Spirit?

We have been given a command by Jesus to go into all the world, preach the Gospel, heal the sick, raise the dead, cast out demons, and make disciples of all nations. Jesus knew we would need *power* to be His witnesses. Our success in this supernatural task requires supernatural power. We cannot witness without the power. Jesus told His disciples they would receive this power when the Holy Spirit came. The baptism of the Holy Spirit is our connection with God's power.

As the early Church grew, the Gospel spread. Churches were established, and leaders were chosen who made new disciples. They received the Holy Spirit, spoke in tongues, and flowed in the gifts, just as those on the day of Pentecost. Signs and wonders followed them. Acts of miracles and healings were proof to the people the Kingdom of God was real and present to meet their needs.

The apostles not only had the truth of the Gospel, but they also had the power of the Gospel. The power of the Holy Spirit was so great the sick were healed as their shadows passed by them. Demons were cast out, and the dead were raised. Jesus baptized His followers in the Holy Spirit, and He baptizes us too.

Although we don't see the Holy Spirit, His evidence is all around us. We don't see the wind, but we can see objects moved by the wind. So it is with the Holy Spirit. He is at work when turmoil turns to peace, sorrow turns to joy, sickness turns to health, and sinfulness turns to righteousness. The greatest working of the Holy Spirit is to lead sinners to the saving knowledge of Jesus Christ.

He bears witness to Jesus and to the Father. He confirms the Word of God, giving us the ability to preach the truth with boldness. He brings believers into the presence of the Father before His throne to worship and adore Jesus. The Holy Spirit makes His presence known as He manifests Himself through His gifts (discussed further in chapter 4). The baptism of the Holy Spirit not only gives us power, but wisdom, direction, knowledge, gifts, fruit, and truth. If we follow the leading of the Holy Spirit and yield to His workings within us, we are living a life in the Spirit.

How Do I Receive the Baptism of the Holy Spirit with Tongues?

This beautiful experience of the baptism in the Holy Spirit is a free gift that can't be earned. We receive the Spirit not by any works, but by faith in the Word of God. Speaking in tongues is the evidence of the baptism in the Holy Spirit. Everything we receive in the Kingdom of God is by *faith* and yielding our free will to God's will. We are Christ's Body, and He is the Head. The Holy Spirit connects the Head (Christ) to the Body (the Church). The Church is not a building or a denomination. We who believe in Jesus are the Church.

To receive the baptism of the Holy Spirit, we must first receive Jesus as our personal Lord and Savior. Jesus is the baptizer into the Holy Spirit. He is unable to baptize us until we receive Him. The primary way Jesus baptizes us into the Holy Spirit is by other Spirit-filled believers laying hands on us and praying. However, there are instances when people are alone with no one to lay hands on them. They seek Jesus earnestly, desiring to be baptized, and He baptizes them with the evidence of speaking in tongues.

In 1981, I received the baptism of the Holy Spirit. I was alone and prayed for two nights. On the third night, I was baptized and spoke in tongues. Some denominations are fearful of this baptism and say it was only for the early Church. But how can that be, if we are to evangelize and preach this Gospel? We need the same power and demonstration of the Kingdom of God as the early disciples did. I understand there is a fear of being deceived and people are naturally skeptical. I also believe the main reason for this hesitancy is Satan. He knows the power of God is released through the Holy Spirit. Once empowered, his kingdom is threatened and torn down. He uses doubt and fear, which causes individuals and entire denominations to refuse this baptism.

I have had doubts many times in my Christian walk. The way I overcame them was to go to God's Word and believe what He says. I came to Christ from a background of mistrust. It was extremely difficult for me to trust God. I loved Jesus, I knew He saved me, and I wanted all He had for me, but I was too fearful to trust Him. I had conversations that went like this: "I can't even see You. How can I trust You, or how do I know if it's You I'm hearing?"

There were two Scriptures that helped me trust God: Luke 11:9-13 and John 10:3-5. We can fully trust our loving heavenly Father to give us His Son and His Holy Spirit. Jesus called us His sheep and told us we would hear His voice. Not just hear His voice, but also follow Him and not a stranger. A stranger is typically a person, but it can also be a strange or false doctrine, devised by the devil, to lead us away from Jesus.

Scriptures are powerful; they're not mere words. They're seed, and when planted in a heart that believes, bear much fruit. As we learn God's character and see Him answer our prayers, we relax and begin to trust Him. It is the beginning of walking by faith. As the years have passed, I trust Him with all my heart. I trust Him with my salvation, my health, my loved ones, my finances, my strengths, and especially with my weaknesses.

I've been through many big battles since my salvation in 1981. God has never forsaken me, never hurt me, never given up on me, and has always provided everything I needed and more. He will do the same for you. Trust Him; He wants to take you further than you ever thought possible. At the end of this chapter, there is a prayer to receive the baptism of the Holy Spirit with speaking in your new prayer language. I encourage you to step out in faith, put your trust in God's Word, and receive.

God admonishes us to pray without ceasing, to pray with perseverance, and to pray effectually. Apart from the Holy Spirit, we can't do this. Our prayers become little more than routine when we pray without the Holy Spirit. Only He can direct us to pray effectually and fervently. It's not within our carnal nature to understand, to intercede, or to agree with the Holy Spirit. We lack the wisdom of how to pray because while we have the mind of Christ, we don't always know the will of Christ.

There are many situations where I don't know what to pray. As I rely on the Holy Spirit to pray through me, it becomes a beautiful union of submission, order, and successful outcome. For instance, when I pray with others I'm at a disadvantage to fully understand their true needs. I hear what they ask, but they might present their need from one position, not identifying the real need. I respectfully listen to their request, but I also listen to the Holy Spirit. As I am praying in tongues, He directs my thoughts. We wouldn't have the knowledge or the advantage to help others apart from the cooperation of the Holy Spirit. I believe prayer is most effective when it's specific. Many prayers go unanswered because the prayer request doesn't address the real need.

A few months ago, I was out shopping. The lady helping me was in a lot of knee pain. I felt the Holy Spirit prompt me, so I asked her if I could pray for her. She said, with much discouragement, "A lot of people have prayed for me." Straightway the Holy Spirit responded through me and I said, "But has anyone believed for you?" She looked amazed at my response. What was her real need at that moment? Yes, it was to have her knee stop hurting, but it was also to overcome her unbelief with the faith she needed for healing. I spoke to her unbelief when I asked if I could *believe* for her healing. Then I spoke to her knee in faith, and the pain was immediately gone. Jesus did the same thing when He addressed the Samaritan woman at the well.

She came to the well because thirst was her immediate need. Jesus saw beyond her immediate need to her real need, which was eternal life. A miraculous exchange occurred. She became the very water jar she had carried to the well. Her real need wasn't a drink of water, but the Water of Life Himself. Now filled with Living Water, she became the first female evangelist to her city. Her thirst was quenched, her salvation secured, and others met Jesus through her encounter with Him. Like this woman, we come with immediate needs and Jesus always supplies both the immediate and the eternal.

Jesus sees beyond what is presented to address what is needed. He not only ministered in the Spirit, but He also saw and listened in the Spirit. My point is this: praying in the Spirit is a more effective way to pray. We don't have to pray alone, struggle with what to ask, how long to ask, or make sure we ask the right thing. We have the person of the Holy Spirit, and we have His help. He leads and reveals all truth. He is the Teacher, the Intercessor, the Helper, and the Paraclete.

The Unpardonable Sin

What does the Bible mean when it says there is no forgiveness for those who commit the unpardonable sin and blaspheme the Holy Spirit? Some think unpardonable sins are murder or sexual sin. But sin is sin to God. There are no big sins or little sins. There is just sin. However, there is one sin that bears the most consequence. There is no pardon for this sin. To commit this sin a person must totally reject the message of the Holy Spirit.

As we've seen in this chapter, the Holy Spirit is the Spirit of Truth. He reveals Jesus to the entire world. He reveals Jesus's death, resurrection, and ascension back to the Father in heaven. He also reveals Jesus's mission to save the world from eternal hell. To deny the message of the Holy Spirit and the truth He brings is to commit blasphemy against Him.

If a person rejects Christ, there is no other atonement. God came once to die for the sins of all mankind. He's not going to the cross again. To blaspheme the Holy Spirit is to blaspheme God Himself. In essence, we call God a liar, and we reject the truth. For that sin, there is no pardon, no forgiveness, no ransom, no advocate, and no intercessor. There is only eternal separation and damnation to hell.

Prayer to Receive the Baptism of the Holy Spirit

Heavenly Father, I recognize my need for Your power to live this new life in Christ. I renounce all works of darkness and any areas of allegiance to Satan. Lord Jesus, You are the baptizer, and I ask You to baptize me right now. I receive this baptism by faith. Please fill me with Your Holy Spirit. Come, Holy Spirit. You are welcome in my life. Teach me how to walk in this baptism for Your glory and for Your Kingdom. Teach me how to use this power and manifest Your gifts through me so I can be Your witness. I also ask You to give me my prayer language right now and teach me about Your gifts so I can help others. In Jesus's name. Amen.

Now fully yield to the Holy Spirit. He will give you the gift of new words (tongues) or utterances. Whatever sounds or words you hear, repeat them. *Step out in faith!* This is your prayer language. You are speaking a new language and not your known language. Thank God, but don't speak in English or a second language. Start to praise God, thank Him, and worship Him.

As an infant learning to speak you made noises. You didn't make sentences or paragraphs. You made sounds. This is the way you will begin when speaking in tongues. Keep practicing. Keep speaking. In a little while, maybe minutes or hours, you will take off and speak more fluently. It is your natural reasoning that holds you back. This language isn't spoken by the brain. It comes from your spirit. It is the Holy Spirit speaking through you to the Father.

Questions

1. Name some attributes of the Holy Spirit. _____
   _____
   _____
   _____

2. What three things does the Holy Spirit convict the world of doing? _____
   _____
   _____
   _____

3. What did Jesus say we would receive when the Holy Spirit comes? _____
   _____
   _____

4. Who baptizes a person in the Holy Spirit? _____

5. When did Jesus send the Holy Spirit to His followers? _____

6. How many people were added to the Church in Jerusalem in one day? _____

7. How does praying in the Spirit help us? _____
   _____
   _____
   _____

8. How did Jesus meet the need of the Samaritan woman at the well? _____
   _____
   _____
   _____

9. What do we have to do to receive the baptism of the Holy Spirit? _____
   _____
   _____
   _____

10. What holds a person back from receiving their prayer language? _____
    _____
    _____
    _____

Reflections: _____
_____
_____
_____
_____
_____
_____
_____
_____
_____
_____
_____

Prayers: _____
_____
_____
_____
_____
_____
_____
_____
_____
_____
_____
_____
_____

Additional Scripture References for Study

Genesis 1:2, Luke 1:41, Luke 3:16-22, Luke 11:9-13, Luke 12:10,
Matthew 3:1-11, John 4:7-30, John 10:3-5, John 14:17, 26, John 20:22,
Acts 1:4-16, Acts 2:1–4, Acts 4:31-33, Acts 5:12–16, Acts 6:5, Acts 8:15-19,
Acts 9:17, Acts 10:38-47, Acts 11:16-24, Acts 15:28, Acts 19:1–7,
Ephesians 5:18, Ephesians 6:18, Galatians 5:25, Romans 8:14-17,
Mark 3:28-30, Matthew 12:31-32

Authority of the Believer

Chapter 2 contains an essential key to healing the sick. We must know who we are in Christ and the authority Jesus has given us to be His witnesses. Not only are we His witnesses, but we also work in cooperation with the Holy Spirit to establish God's Kingdom here on earth. We've been entrusted with the Gospel of Jesus Christ. As such, we have the message the world needs to hear. In His Kingdom, we've been given authority and access to His power over the enemy. We've been given authority to tear down strongholds of sickness and disease and to set people free in Christ. Careful attention to this chapter demonstrates who we are in Christ and enables us to take our place of position in the Body of Christ. Following salvation, our next step is to learn and understand our authority in Christ as believers.

CHAPTER 2

Authority of the Believer

Healing the sick by faith requires not only the power of the Holy Spirit, but also His authority. *Authority* is given to all believers the moment they first put trust in Christ as Lord and Savior.[3] The instant you are born again you have the name, the blood, and the authority of Christ to reign with Him. *Power* comes when you receive the baptism of the Holy Spirit. Many Christians don't walk in their Kingdom rights of authority and power because many churches don't teach these truths. I believe this is because the enemy wars against any such advancement of God's Kingdom here on earth. Jesus gave His disciples authority and power over the devil, to heal the sick, and to cast out demons.

Jesus has given you this same authority. You may be a new Christian just learning the Bible. Even though your knowledge of God's Word is limited, you have His authority the same as a seasoned Christian who has walked with Christ for years and studied His Word. When I came to Christ, I came from a liturgical denomination that didn't teach or interpret the Word of God, nor was there an emphasis on memorizing Scripture. My conversion stirred up the enemy's camp, and the demonic attacks were intense.

I was awakened one particular morning by a very evil presence in my bedroom. I was so afraid, I could hardly breathe. Not knowing how to pray, I remembered the first verse of Psalm 23, which I had learned in public school. I said it out loud and immediately the evil presence moved away from me. I said it again and again until it was gone. That was my first encounter with my authority in the name of Jesus and in His Word.

I didn't know the Holy Spirit was teaching me spiritual warfare, but as the weeks and months went on, I quickly learned I had Jesus's authority over the enemy. I was only

---

[3] John MacMillan, *Authority of the Believer* (Camp Hills, PA: WingSpread Publishers, 2007).

a couple of weeks old in the baptism of the Holy Spirit and knew very little Scripture. However, authority over the enemy was my Kingdom right. I could speak against the attack of the devil, quote Scripture, use the name of Jesus, and be victorious!

As Christians grow in Christ, the Holy Spirit teaches and reveals Scripture. In this process, we learn how to use our authority in Christ. Apart from Jesus, we have no authority or power. Not knowing what belongs to us doesn't activate or negate the truth. I can be an heir to a fortune but never claim it. I must first know I'm an heir, then claim the gift. The devil not only fears the heirs but also dreads their inheritance because it roots out his evil workings and establishes the Kingdom of God. We are to use the authority God has given us, through His Son, Jesus Christ. It's the authority of every believer, given by God, to not only do the works Jesus did, but also do greater works than His because He went back to heaven and is seated at the right hand of God.

When you walk in the authority Christ has given you, the devil will tempt and challenge you. He usually starts by planting seeds of doubt regarding your salvation and God's forgiveness of your sins. If he can get you to doubt your salvation, you'll never advance to your position of authority over him. If his condemnation over past sins is successful, you'll never stand in the victory of what Jesus died to give you.

You must settle these issues once and for all. Assurance of salvation and forgiveness come from the Word of God. Remember, Jesus stripped the devil of all power and authority as the god of this world. The only power he has is the power you give him through not knowing God's Word and promises. The following Scripture references are to defend your salvation with assurance in what Christ has done:

> **Romans 10:9-10 (KJV)**
> **⁹ That if thou shalt confess with thy mouth the Lord Jesus, and shalt believe in thine heart that God hath raised him from the dead, thou shalt be saved. ¹⁰ For with the heart man believeth unto righteousness; and with the mouth confession is made unto salvation.**

> **Ephesians 2:8 (KJV)**
> **For by grace are ye saved through faith; and that not of yourselves: it is the gift of God:**

> **John 3:16-18 (KJV)**
> **¹⁶ For God so loved the world that he gave his only begotten Son, that whosoever believeth in him should not perish, but have everlasting life. ¹⁷ For God sent not his Son into the world to condemn the world; but that the world through him might be saved. ¹⁸ He that believeth on him is not**

condemned: but he that believeth not is condemned already, because he hath not believed in the name of the only begotten Son of God.

1 John 1:9 (KJV)
If we confess our sins, he is faithful and just to forgive us our sins and to cleanse us from all unrighteousness.

Back to the Beginning

In studying the Christian's authority, it's helpful to see that the origin of our authority began at creation. The book of Genesis tells of a beginning, a time when there was nothing but darkness. From that darkness, God created the heavens, the earth, the plants, and the animals. Then He created man in His image and likeness and placed him in Eden, God's garden. His creation was spectacular in design, order, and purpose. Man wasn't created to live a life like the animals. God gave him authority, power, and dominion to rule over all He created. God's unique design for man was to rule with authority and power in the earth:

Psalm 115:16 (KJV)
The heaven, even the heavens, are the LORD's: but the earth hath He given to the children of men.

Adam and Eve lived in a perfect garden with perfect purpose until the day they disobeyed God's commandment. How tragic one single decision became and how devastating its effect. All that had been perfect was instantly lost. The rights, the dominion, and the purity of a sinless life were swallowed up in a moment of rebellion and sin. God, the Righteous Judge, could not overlook the offense. There was a penalty for disobedience, a debt to be paid, and the price was death.

There in the garden, light fell away to darkness; presence was removed by distance. The flimsy, makeshift covering of their nakedness gave way to the first blood sacrifice as God wrapped the couple in animal skins. Imagine, all that had been peace was now chaos. All that had been security was turned into anxiety and intimacy was replaced by rejection. God is pure and holy. Sin separates us from Him. There was no sin up to the time they disobeyed God. There was grace and fellowship with God (Elohim), their Creator.

I've found my answer as I've pondered why God, who knows all things, allowed the forbidden fruit on the tree, the command not to eat it, and the devil into the garden. God could have left the couple in paradise with no temptation, but He chose to create man higher than any other creature. God gave man far more superiority over the earth than any of the creatures on the earth. While all creation had instinct and limitation, God gave man two extraordinary gifts: the ability to reason for himself, and a free will.

God extended the ultimate trust in order to teach man to trust Him. The forbidden fruit, the command, and the tempter were given by design. God intended those three things to be tools in growing man to a position of authority and dominion. Trust is the foundation of intimacy and a pillar to every successful relationship. Man was created to reign, not with independent sovereignty, but rather in dependent partnership with God Himself.

The Rebellion That Led to the Fall

Before the fall of Adam and Eve, there'd been another rebellion, one of epic proportion. A third of heaven's host warred in mutiny against God, led by the chief angel, Lucifer. His name and description are listed in two separate accounts of the Old Testament. Ezekiel and Isaiah tell of this angel (Lucifer) who was full of wisdom and perfect in beauty. Called the anointed cherub that covers and protects, he was adorned with precious jewels and gold.

The prophet Isaiah called him Lucifer (light). Jesus called him Satan (adversary). Reading the two Old Testament accounts, you see his creation, his purpose, his rebellion, and his fall. The books give an image of how he looked, where he had access, and the evil within his heart.

Lucifer rebelled against God. He became full of pride and sought to sit on the throne of God. When he was cast out of heaven his name changed from *light to adversary*. Satan, now defeated by God, turned his wrath against God's highest creation, Adam. God had created Adam and Eve in His image and likeness, giving them dominion to rule and reign in the earth. In his rebellion against God, Satan set out to make mankind rebels in his image and likeness. Being the thief and the destroyer that he is, Satan began his assault against humanity. He came to steal what God had given, and he continues to be the thief today.

An outcast from heaven, he sought to make mankind outcasts along with him. He would use the same sins of pride, arrogance, and rebellion he had used against God. He was no match for God, but he was a match for Adam and Eve. If he could persuade them to believe God's command was a lie, they would disobey God. When they ate the fruit, their fate was sealed. Satan knew firsthand the consequence of rebellion and sin. He was living testimony of what disobedience could produce. In his hatred for God, he turned his wrath against God's creation. Once his lie was believed, the sin was committed. In that moment dominion, authority, and privilege ceased. What had been Adam's position of power in the earth fell under the control of Satan. As long as man obeyed Satan and disobeyed God, *he* would be their god.

Cast Away

Eden became the place of ruin, the place of betrayal and disobedience, the place of mankind's fall from grace. Just as Lucifer had rebelled against God, he replicated his actions upon our first parents. As God pronounced judgments on all three, beginning with the serpent, He also pronounced His mercy and grace. He foretold of His great plan to redeem man back to Himself. In the heart of God, in the sorrow of the moment, He spoke of redemption. Adam and Eve could have never imagined the severity of their disobedience. It would have crushed them to know the extent of the consequences of their sin. Not only had they sinned, but they had also cut themselves off from God, and there was no way to redeem the loss.

Access back into the garden was sealed. They were cast away from Eden, but more tragically they were cast away from the presence of God. Their sin brought death and permanent separation from God. Not only were they separated from God, but they were also separated from wisdom, provision, and fellowship. Spiritually blind, they were separated with no possible way to recover. Just as God had warned them they would surely die, their same judgment fell on all mankind.

From the beginning of time to Christ's return, everyone is born spiritually blind and spiritually dead in sin. The good news of the Gospel is this: Jesus came for the dead. He came to make a way for all to return to God; to make us alive in Him, to be born again anew, restored, and redeemed. Jesus said we must be born again, not of flesh but of the Spirit. Born again because we were born spiritually blind and we live spiritually dead. Once we receive Him as Savior and Lord, we are resurrected from death and hell to life and union with God. Our eyes are opened to truth, and our spirit lives because Jesus is the Resurrection and the Life.

A good example of our own spiritual blindness might be explained this way. I've worn glasses for twenty years. If I lose or misplace my glasses I not only lose my sight, but I also lose the ability to find my glasses and regain my sight. I need my eyesight to help me find my glasses, but having lost my glasses, I have lost my eyesight! So it was for our first parents. They needed fellowship with God to have perfect vision and purpose. When they sinned, they lost fellowship with God, like losing a pair of glasses. Not only did they lose their relationship with God, but they also lost the ability to find it again.

With their vision gone, there was no way to recover, no way back to paradise. They were without God and had no way to return. Their wisdom, provision, purpose, position, and authority were lost. God had warned disobedience would bring death. All humanity would be plunged into sin and death because of Adam and Eve's disobedience. All of us are born dead in our trespasses. All of us are lost in the sense of needing vision, and none of us have a way back to God on our own. We are blind and spiritually dead. Lost in sin, we needed someone to come and get us. So God Himself came for us. The One who created us, who loves us, came to rescue us. He made a way back for us.

God's Redemption through His Son, Jesus Christ

Our rescuer is God Himself. At just the right time, according to His plan of redemption, He came to earth to lead us home. The price for our sin debt was so high no amount of animal blood could wipe out our transgressions. Like the covering of animal skins God made for Adam and Eve, the law of Moses only made provision for covering offenses. It never provided a cleansing from all unrighteousness. That degree of cleanliness could only be satisfied with God's blood that was shed for us. He is the perfect lamb, sinless and spotless. He came of His own free will with a heart to purchase us.

All of us; every sin, every fault, and every offense was paid by His blood. He came in flesh and blood to give His blood as payment for our sins. The work on Calvary's cross culminated in the transference of sin and guilt, curse and eternal damnation to love; love that not only covers us but also changes us into a new creation in Christ. Love changes every heart that will trust and believe God. Jesus saved us from the wrath of God and met the demand and payment for our sin. He paid the world's debt. He surrendered to the humiliation of the cross. God Himself, having left the glory and splendor of heaven, was stripped and beaten, cursed and crucified, so that we might have freedom and eternal life.

We were enemies of God, deserving death, but Jesus in His kindness died so we might be reconciled back to the Father. The gift is too extraordinary for mere human words. His love rescued us. Jesus not only took our sin, but He also gave us His righteousness. That righteousness came with His power, His authority, and His dominion. Once again, we've been reinstated through Christ to rule and reign on the earth. God does not rescind His purposes. They stand even in the face of man's wickedness and rebellion. God created us to rule and reign on this earth. Now in Christ, we have authority to establish His Kingdom on earth.

The First Man, Adam; the Second Man, Christ

The Old Testament is filled with prophecies pointing to a savior who would redeem Israel. There were two men, Adam and Christ, in two gardens, Eden and Gethsemane. Eden was a delightful garden, a prepared place fashioned for God's highest creation. Gethsemane was also a prepared place. Located in the Kidron Valley, the Mount of Olives stood over ancient grounds that contained the broken and burned pieces of Old Testament idols. Wicked kings of Israel had erected monuments to false gods in betrayal to their true God.

When King Asa, King Hezekiah, and King Josiah rose to power, they tore down Judah and Israel's idols, piling up the destroyed remnants in the Kidron Valley. Jeremiah the prophet had looked out over this abhorrent desolation and prophesied that there was a day coming when this place would be called holy. It was here that Jesus's first drops of blood fell in the midst of the garden before His betrayal. When Adam sinned, God pronounced a curse to the ground under his feet. Jesus's blood fell on the ground and immediately the curse was removed.

Jesus had entered the garden many times to pray. Soon He would be pressed and crushed like the fruit of its trees. The finest oil poured out for our salvation. Eden had been the place of rebellion and betrayal where the first man, Adam, committed treason against God. Gethsemane was the place Jesus bowed before His Father in obedience and submission to His will. Adam's hands had toiled in the heat of the day, producing thorns and thistles. The head of our Savior was pierced and bore the crown fashioned from the curse that belonged to Adam. Gethsemane's ground received the first cleansing blood of Jesus.

As His blood spilled, what once was cursed became holy, fulfilling the prophet Jeremiah's words. Adam lost his position of honor; Jesus laid His position down. Adam toiled and worked for bread, but heaven's bread, Jesus, came to save the world. Adam's punishment was deserved, but Jesus was innocent of any sin and obediently took our punishment. Adam was cast out of Eden, but Jesus came of His own free will into Gethsemane. Satan tempted Adam in Eden and defeated him, but when he came to tempt Jesus in Gethsemane, he was defeated. Adam took counsel from Satan in Eden, but Jesus took counsel with His Father in Gethsemane. An angel appeared in both Eden and Gethsemane. One tempted, accused, lied, and deceived. The other obeyed, comforted, and strengthened.

From Calvary's cross, Jesus declared His work was finished. He had done what He came to do, which was to destroy the works of the devil. His death and resurrection forever stripped Satan of his authority. Jesus conquered sin and death, took our punishment, and forever paid our debt with His own precious blood. All power and authority have been given to Jesus. Man's need for Christ isn't only to obtain eternal salvation. It is also to continue the work of Jesus and to establish God's Kingdom here on earth until He returns.

Authority and Power Restored by Faith in Christ

Jesus secured our rightful authority and dominion through His death and resurrection. The believer's part is to step into His provision by faith. Authority as a believer began the moment we received Christ as our Lord and Savior. At our new birth, we were given Kingdom rights, privileges, and power over the enemy. Our faith in Christ makes us joint heirs with Jesus. As believers, we were also given Kingdom purposes. Authority isn't a special gift given to the chosen few. All believers have been endowed with this authority through Christ's authority.

The Holy Spirit teaches us how to effectively use it for the advancement of God's Kingdom on earth. The coming of the Holy Spirit into a person's life doesn't give the believer authority. Authority came when the believer received Christ as Lord and Savior. The coming of the Holy Spirit into a believer's life gives them power. It's the power of God that produces miracles, leads a sinner to repentance, changes a hardened heart, and brings about the new birth. The Holy Spirit manifests through the believer as He wills, with powerful gifts, which include healing and miracles. These gifts are discussed at length in chapter 4 of this book.

Weapons of Our Warfare

Just as every soldier is trained to know and fire his weapon for the day of battle, the same is true of every believer. Our weapons are not physical or visible, but they are mighty to the pulling down of strongholds. The weapons of our warfare have been confused with the fruit of the Spirit, but that isn't the arsenal Paul speaks of in 2 Corinthians. Fruit is not a weapon against the enemy, but rather the hallmark of a mature Christian. Our weapon of warfare is the Gospel of Jesus Christ. It is the truth revealed in the good news of Christ's deity and dominion.

These weapons (these truths) are mighty to the pulling down of strongholds and the destruction of the enemy's lies and deceit. The Word is more powerful than a two-edged sword. Jesus used it to defeat Satan in the wilderness. Professing religion will not defeat the devil, nor does it assure one of eternal life. Unless there is true conversion, evidenced by the fruit of repentance, religion is only a form of godliness, void of power and ineffective against the devil. Once a person receives Jesus as Lord, there must be growth through studying and living the Word of God.

A disciple is a follower of Christ who puts all his faith and trust in Jesus. He believes God's Word and lays down his own will to take up the will of God. It's a dying to self and living for Christ. Through this obedience the Holy Spirit teaches us how to use the Word as a deadly weapon against Satan. Our authority and power come from the Word of God. Knowing it and using it effectively, we can tear down the strongholds of the enemy and set the captives free in Christ.

Seated in Christ

Our position of authority is in Christ, who is seated at the right hand of the Father. He sits now until the time, known only to the Father, when He will come again for His Church.

Jesus sits over all principalities, power, might, and dominion. He sits as head over all things. Head over the Body, which is His Church, made up of true believers. Jesus sits far above all dominion, far above every name that is named, not only in this age, but also in the age to come.

Jesus sits, having completely stripped all the mighty principalities and powers. He holds the keys to death and hell. In Christ, we're not only set free from the punishment of sin, but we're also entitled to receive every spiritual blessing in heaven, because we are sanctified in Christ and made holy in the sight of God. It's from this heavenly position in Christ that we are given authority and power to rule and reign. We are on assignment to establish God's Kingdom here on earth.

Humble Boldness

Based on our knowledge of the Word of God, knowing the agony of the cross, the shedding of His blood for the atonement of our sins, the redemption of mankind, the restoration of creation to the Creator, the cancellation of our debt, the resurrection of Christ, and His place at the Father's right hand, how can we possibly think we could do anything to contribute to Jesus's perfect and complete work? It's with humility of heart we so deeply love Christ for coming to save us.

We come before Jesus in meekness, assured of His great love and mercy for us. In this redemption, Jesus gives us His authority and power to act as His representatives here on earth. We're His Body, and He is our Head. Our boldness lies in the finished work of the cross. At the hour of His death, the curtain into the Holy of Holies, where His Shekinah glory manifested once a year, was torn from the top down to the bottom, thus signifying there was no longer a separation between unholy people and a righteous God.

We have access to the throne room of God through Christ and Christ alone. Into the very presence of Almighty God not as a slave, fearful for our lives, but as adopted sons and daughters. Whatever our need, through Christ, we have complete access to God because we are redeemed and made righteous before Him in Christ. God is no longer wrathful and judgmental towards the ones who have received the work of His Son in reconciliation. He is gracious and merciful, kind and patient.

We can be confident God draws near when we approach Him in humility. Our authority is activated in the name of Jesus. When we speak the Word of God, we speak according to the will of God. When we speak, we tear down strongholds, topple kingdoms, and establish God's Kingdom here on earth. As believers, we must continually renew our minds in the Word of God, continually dwell in His presence and in His fellowship, listen and discern the voice of the Holy Spirit, and act on the directives we are given. It is in His name and what He has done that we take our rightful place of humble boldness, giving all the glory to Jesus.

Where Are the Boundary Lines?

To what degree does our authority and power extend? Where are the boundary lines? All things have boundaries, even in the Kingdom of heaven. Our authority is over the power of the enemy, not over the free will of others.[4] God has given each of us the power of free will. We choose to obey and serve or disobey and rebel. God will never send anyone to hell. Each of us will make the choice of heaven or hell. God never forces His will on us.

Heaven awaits those who know they're sinners, have repented, and made Jesus their Lord and Savior. Hell awaits those who know they're sinners, are unrepentant, and have rejected the gift of salvation in Jesus Christ. If God gives us such a great free will, we have no right, power, or authority to control the will of anyone else. The believer is given authority and power for the purpose of defeating the enemy and aiding in the release of the captives. Jesus died that we may be free, and in that freedom, free others caught in the trap of sin and death.

Binding and Loosing

When Jesus asked His disciples who they thought He was, their answers were Elijah or John. Peter spoke up with amazing revelation and proclaimed Jesus to be the Messiah (Christ). We all receive the same revelation truth Peter received when we are born again. We are the Church, the Body of Christ, built on the foundational truth that Jesus is our Savior. Jesus, on hearing Peter's revelation, gave him the keys to the Kingdom of heaven.

Keys are made for locking and unlocking. They are descriptive of *authority* and *power*. Owners entrust keys to those delegated to act on their behalf. Keys have the power to open and close doors, and in this reference by Jesus, to loosen (open) and to bind (close). Keys also confer the believer's authority and power from God, acting as His representative, in accordance with the spiritual laws already set in place. Along with His authority and power, there must come submission and obedience. We are to carry out the assignment, as heaven deems lawful and just. The keys are not a means to self-assertion, self-will, and self-direction, but rather a means of subjection to the Holy Spirit.

Moses received the law on Mount Sinai four thousand years before Jesus came to earth. When disputes arose among the Jews, they went to the rabbi for interpretation and resolution. The rabbi would sanction (loose) it or bind (forbid) it according to the teachings

---

[4] John MacMillan, *Authority of the Believer* (Camp Hills, PA: WingSpread Publishers, 2007).

of the Torah.[5] According to Sid Roth: "The people to whom He spoke understood that He was talking about what was consistent with Torah and what wasn't. This matter of binding and loosing wasn't unique to Yeshua. It was entirely familiar to them all because it was how the rabbis would sanction something or ban it according to the teachings in Torah."[6]

When Jesus spoke of binding and loosing, they were terms Peter and the disciples completely understood. Even though Peter would have been familiar with Jesus's terminology, I believe he was somewhat puzzled as to why Jesus would confer authority on him.

Peter was not a Levitical priest or a member of the Sanhedrin, so why would Jesus confer the rabbinical authority of a priest onto him, a disciple of Messiah? Jesus was ending His earthly ministry and going to the cross. In this discourse with Peter, He was setting the wheels in motion for the coming of the Holy Spirit and the New Testament Church. In less than two months Pentecost would arrive, birthing the Body of Christ by adding, in one day, three thousand new members.

Peter would lead the New Testament Jerusalem Church. Jesus was conferring *authority* over Church matters onto Peter, giving him the keys of the Kingdom of heaven. Not only did Jesus give Peter the keys, but He also told him his authority must line up with what heaven already held to be legal (allowable), or illegal (unallowable).

Binding and loosing are powerful keys when healing the sick. As believers, we have the same authority to declare things lawful or unlawful in accordance with what heaven has called lawful and unlawful. Heaven doesn't back up our misinterpretation of God's Word. We must line up with heaven's authority. God wants us healthy, so it must be lawful to be healed! If there's no sickness in heaven and we pray for God's will to be done on earth as it's done in heaven, what are we saying? We are forbidding and declaring sickness to be unlawful and unpermitted here, just as it is forbidden and declared unlawful in heaven.

Jesus did this each time He healed the sick, raised the dead, and cast out demons. He established Kingdom laws here on earth. We are to do the same. Sickness and disease have attached themselves where they have no legal right. Satan uses stolen authority to attack us. There's no sickness or disease in heaven. Therefore, if God's will be done on earth as it is done in heaven, then we have authority to forbid (bind) them from a person.

---

[5] Sid Roth "Binding, Loosing, Torah & Power," February 16, 2012, from the web page of Sid Roth's It's Supernatural. Used by permission by Messianic Vision, www.sidroth.org, 2016, https://sidroth.org/articles/binding-loosing-torah-power/.
[6] Ibid.

Things unlawful or forbidden in the Kingdom of heaven are: sickness, disease, poverty, darkness, demonic activity, fear, unbelief, lies, deceptions, rebellion, pride, and sin. Things lawful or permitted in the Kingdom of heaven are: salvation, healing, restoration, wholeness, peace, life, grace, love, forgiveness, and the Word of God.

If it is lawful and permitted in the Kingdom of heaven, and the Kingdom of heaven is within each believer, then we have the same authority here on earth as the apostles had. This authority and power allow us to have dominion over unclean spirits and cast them out; to heal every kind of sickness and disease, to destroy the works of the devil, and establish the Kingdom of God here on earth.

A more effective way to pray is to bind the *plan* of the enemy and to loose the *will* of God. We rebuke sickness, disease, and poverty because they are Old Testament curses and we command the abundant life Jesus died to give us in John 10:10. We have Jesus's authority to cancel the enemy's assignments and to call his plans to nothing. I wake up each morning and take my authority in Christ over the day. I say and declare these words:

> *Devil, in the name of Jesus, I take authority over your plan to kill, steal, and destroy today. You will not execute your plan over me, my family, or any of the things I have been given in Christ. I speak to that plan of yours and curse it and call it to nothing, in the name of Jesus Christ. I bind it and send it away. Father, I take my authority in Christ for Your will to be done. You have a good plan for us to walk in today. I loose that plan and speak life and blessings over this day. Thy Kingdom come, Thy will be done, in the name of Jesus. Show me who I can help today, who You want to reach through me. Let that plan be released over us today. In Jesus's name. Amen.*

Questions

1. Write one Scripture confirming your salvation. _____
    _____
    _____
    _____

2. What three things did God give Adam and Eve in the garden? _____
    _____
    _____

3. Besides God, who else had access to the garden with Adam and Eve? _____
    _____

4. At what point in our salvation did we receive authority in the name of Jesus? _____
    _____

5. What are the weapons of our warfare? _____
    _____
    _____

6. Our authority has limits. Who do we not have authority over? _____
    _____

7. The terms binding and loosing refer to what two terms? _____
    _____
    _____

8. Who received the keys to the Kingdom of heaven? _____

9. How many people were saved in one day in Jerusalem on Pentecost? _____

10. In Matthew 10:1, what did Jesus send out His disciples to do? _____
    _____
    _____
    _____

Reflections: _____
_____
_____
_____
_____
_____
_____
_____
_____
_____
_____
_____

Prayers: _____
_____
_____
_____
_____
_____
_____
_____
_____
_____
_____
_____

Additional Scripture References for Study

Revelation 3:20, Romans 1:16, John 10:27-29, John 3:16, Genesis 1:26-28,
Ezekiel 28:13-18, Isaiah 14:12-15, Acts 4:10-12, 2 Peter 2:4, Luke 10:18-20,
John 8:36, Hebrews 4:14-16, Numbers 23:19, Romans 11:29, Colossians 3:1,
2 Corinthians 10:3-5, Hebrews 4:12-16, Romans 6:20-23, Matthew 10:1,
Matthew 16:13-21, Ephesians 2:4-8, Jeremiah 31: 38-40, 2 Kings 22: 1-23, Luke 9:1

Hearing the Voice of God

Chapter 3 emphasizes the relationship we have with the Holy Spirit as we learn to listen and discern His voice. Healing the sick is impossible apart from the working of the Holy Spirit. To be led by Him we must be able to hear and recognize His voice. As vessels with a free will, we operate in partnership submitting to the will of God. Hearing is vital for success. As we learn to discern God's voice, we can flow and move as the Holy Spirit directs. He will help us and train us to hear. When praying for others, this is key to unlocking the chains that bind them. It's imperative we speak the things we hear Him say. God's voice is heard through our spirit, not through our ears.

CHAPTER 3

Hearing the Voice of God

Hearing the voice of God in every area of our life is one of the keys to living in success. Hearing the voice of God when ministering healing is crucial to achieving success. I make it a practice to listen to the person who needs healing and listen to the Holy Spirit. While we may be able to discern branches, God knows the root or heart of a situation. God not only knows the root of the issue, but He also addresses and deals with it. I solely depend on the Holy Spirit for discernment and wisdom in ministering healing to others and as such, have seen great results.

God continually communicates with us. We were created to depend on Him and to be led and directed by Him. Our sinful nature manifests as we seek to follow our own way, solve our own problems, and direct our own life. The natural man sees no problem with this type of independent thinking because he lacks the wisdom of God. The world itself, governed by the god of this world, enforces the belief of independence from God. This is very dangerous. We don't have God's wisdom, and we don't realize we lack the wisdom necessary to live a successful life. This wisdom only comes as we seek God.

The first step to hearing God is to admit we need Him. The second step is to obey Him. We must turn from self-reliance to relying entirely on the Holy Spirit. The third step is to seek God's wisdom and guidance in every decision and circumstance we encounter. God will never scold us when we seek Him for wisdom. He wants us to come to Him, seek Him, and seek His will and His plan. He will generously and freely give wisdom to anyone who asks.

Purpose Ourselves to Hear the Voice of God

To purpose something is to be deliberate about it. We can purpose ourselves to hear God in several ways: through His Word, through doctrinal teaching, through spending time with the Holy Spirit, and through fellowshipping with other Christians. We cannot hear the voice of God through the world's system of communication. I didn't hear or recognize the voice of God until I received the baptism of the Holy Spirit with speaking in tongues.

As I prayed in the Spirit and asked the Holy Spirit for the interpretation of tongues, I became familiar with the voice of God. Submission is also another way we purpose to hear God's voice. As I hear His voice and obey His direction, He opens more and more communication to me. Why would God continue to speak if we have purposed not to listen or obey?

Simply believing God exists and knowing Jesus died for our sins are not enough. We must submit our lives to Him and obey Him. He must become Lord over our lives. Devils believe God exists, but they have not submitted to Him; nor do they give Jesus lordship. Jesus must become our personal Lord. He is the only way to salvation. We must receive His death and His forgiveness for our sins. Jesus paid our debt. If God went to all this trouble to save us, don't you think He wants to communicate with us? Of course He does. God has given each person a free will, and He won't violate that gift. It's our choice to seek after God with all our heart or to ignore Him.

I often say, "If we take one step toward turning to God, He takes a thousand steps to meet us." Moses purposed himself to *turn aside* and take a step toward God. When he did, his whole life changed. Not only his life, but also the lives of the Egyptians, Pharaoh, and all the children of Israel. God is constantly reaching out to us, desiring us to live the life He created for us. We have a free will and the ability to choose whether to respond to Him or go our own way. Our seeking God should be consistent every day, not just in our time of crisis and need. The majority of people to whom you will minister healing are in a crisis and unable to hear God's voice. A lot of how we minister healing is to reinforce God's unconditional love and acceptance of them through the person of Jesus Christ.

Recently I prayed with a frail, elderly woman. She had problems with her spine and was in a lot of pain. As I laid hands on her back and took authority over sickness and disease, she began to cry. I finished praying and I asked her if the pain was gone. She looked at me and said, "No." The moment you ask a person if their pain is gone and they say, "No," the devil will attack you with their unbelief. I replied, "That's OK."

I put my hands on her back again. When I did the Holy Spirit showed me that she had a "spirit of rejection." I said to her, "You think God has rejected you, don't you? You think that He doesn't hear you or answer you because He is not pleased with you, don't you?"

She said very softly, "Yes." I began to tell her that not only was she loved by God and redeemed by Jesus, but that she was also His beloved. I spent a few more minutes ministering His love to her. Then I asked her to move and see if her back still hurt. She was able to move and be free from the spirit of rejection.

God wants to speak to us. He wants to reveal His Word and His plan for our lives. He also wants us to follow as He works out His wonderful plan. That sounds logical, doesn't it? However, a common mistake we make is to put the context of what God is saying into our limited ability to comprehend what He means. Our ability to understand is somewhat based on our experiences. It is why we look for God to work things out the way He did in the past. He wants to do a new thing. One thing I know about God, He is the Creator, not the repeater!

Our natural tendency is to look at *our* knowledge to interpret *His* Word. Thinking we know what God means, we strike out alone to fulfill what He told us. Abraham and Sarah proved this point. They received a word from God that although barren, Sarah would conceive a child. But the promise was delayed. When promises are delayed, the human tendency is to take control and make things happen. This usually has disastrous consequences as it did with Hagar the bondwoman (slave) and her son Ishmael. God has perfect seasons and perfect timing. We need to train ourselves to not only hear from God but to also wait for His instructions, being careful to walk with Him and continually seek Him. We need to go from doing what is natural to doing what is supernatural.

> *Holy Spirit, I desire with all my heart to hear Your voice. Teach me to listen and to discern Your voice above all other voices in my life. As I pray and as I read the Bible, let Your voice speak to me and make me understand what You are saying. Help me turn away from the distractions of this world so that I can hear You clearly. I bind every voice, including my own, and I forbid them to speak, in the name of Jesus. Do not let me be deceived, but give me Your wisdom and Your voice. In Jesus's name. Amen.*

Trust

The foundation of every good relationship is trust. In the garden of Eden, Satan sought to undermine God by deceiving Adam and Eve. The motive behind his lie was to get the couple to doubt and distrust God. His tactics are the same today. The devil never changes. He tempted Jesus with doubt in hopes He too would disobey. Satan knew without the cross, there would be no crown; without the suffering, there would be no seat of power; without obedience, no redemption; and without death, no resurrection.

God is constantly working with us to establish *trust,* while the enemy constantly works in opposition. Satan's goals are doubt, distrust, and disobedience. Trust is the bedrock of our relationship with God. If a foundation erodes, the structure collapses. If trust is eroded, there will be no intimacy and no obedience. The devil knows this and wars against our trusting God. Trust is a difficult thing for many people. By the time they come to Christ they have experienced so much mistrust that they find it hard to trust God.

Trust is necessary to enter the Kingdom of God because faith is rooted in trust. Unfortunately, a lot of what we do in this Christian life questions the voice of God. *Is that really You, Lord?* This is partly because we don't want to be led astray and partly from our own fearful and doubting hearts. Even when we get God's clear and direct communication, our natural tendency is to sift through our own doubt and unbelief before coming to complete trust.

Jesus called this heart condition a *hardened heart.* He used children as an illustration of what's necessary to enter the Kingdom of God. Unless we have the same level of trust a child has, we cannot enter. When we purpose to trust God, we'll hear Him more clearly. *Mistrust is FEAR. Trust is LOVE.* Fear doesn't come from God; it comes because we don't trust and rely on God. We are more focused on self and reasoning than on trust and love. The opposite of love is not hate; it is fear.

You can trust God. He will never harm you and only desires good for His creation. So how do you learn to trust God? By reading the Bible and renewing your mind in His Word. By believing what He says, He means. The Bible is also the place where you find the love of God, and when you find the love of God, the fear of God no longer exists. God wants you to recognize His voice. He also wants you to distinguish between His voice and other voices. God wants to lead you, and He wants you to follow.

If you are born again, you are His sheep, and you hear His voice. You may not recognize it just yet, but as you trust the Holy Spirit, you will hear. He dwells in your spirit. He is always communicating with you, leading you to Jesus. Trust is the key to resting in the Father's perfect love. He doesn't want you to blindly stumble through life. Over and over in His Word, He says He wants to lead you.

Our heavenly Father is the giver of all good gifts, the best being His only begotten Son. Jesus is the gift and the only way to the Father. In the moment you receive Him as Lord and Savior, you receive eternal life. Your sins are forgiven, and you're made into a new creation. When God the Father sees you, He sees His Son living in your heart, and He is pleased to give you His Kingdom. That might sound like a radical statement to you, but it's because the world doesn't have a full understanding of the radical work of Christ on the cross, the work of redemption.

Hindrances to Hearing God Speak

The number one hindrance to hearing God's voice is the lack of quietness and stillness in our lives. We must purposefully turn off the world. Carve out time in our day that belongs solely to God. We rarely take the time to be still and quiet ourselves because we're too busy. We have an appetite for *more*—more ways to be productive; more ways to do things faster. More things, like big houses, fancier cars, and more jobs to pay for it all. We fall into bed each night exhausted, only to have the clock go off early and start the business all over again.

I believe more is no longer more. In fact, I think more means increasingly less: less time with God, less time with family, less time to be at peace, and less contentment. I am older now and have left the acquisition mode, as I like to call my younger years. All those things I acquired have to be cleaned, dusted, repaired, stored, and finally discarded. Things that seemed so important really don't matter all that much. Jesus's days were busy and active, yet He knew the importance of time alone with God.

One day, Jesus was in the home of Martha, Mary, and Lazarus. They were sisters and brother, and they were friends of Jesus. A crowd had gathered because He was there. Martha was busy preparing food, but Mary, her sister, sat at Jesus's feet, listening intently to His teaching. Martha needed help and complained to Jesus about her sister. Because Jesus loved her so much, He took the opportunity to speak to her heart, pinpointing an area of stress by telling her she was a worrier.

I'd like to think Martha and I have some things in common. We are the fixers, the taskers, the doers, and the worriers. Sometimes we need to stop and come into the presence of Jesus, sit at His feet, and calm down! Again, we must purpose to push the world away, get alone, and tune into the voice of God. God isn't in competition with the world; He is above all things. The heavens and the earth declare His glory, but if we're constantly distracted the world becomes a small sphere, unproductive, filled with self, never nourished, and always lost.

Another hindrance to hearing God is disobedience. When God speaks, we must act on that Word. When we act on that Word, God gives us the next piece to the puzzle. Little by little and step-by-step, as we obey, we learn how to hear and obey. In 2000, God called Jim and me to start a nonprofit corporation. God did not lay out an eighteen-year plan with a day-to-day calendar. As we sought God, He gave us the next step. As we obeyed, we saw success. This developed a trust in God that He would give us what we needed. We learned to lean on Him and obey Him.

It is freeing to depend on the Lord. After all, it's His work in us, His provision to us, and His glory through us. I have not found any biblical account of God laying out His entire plan for someone's life. He absolutely has a plan for every person, but that plan requires something on our part and something on God's part. He gives us what we need to know. After we accomplish that (are obedient to do what He says) He gives the next set of instructions. The key is to listen and obey.

Ways in Which God Speaks to Us

God speaks to us in a number of ways. He is a spirit and communicates through our spirit. His voice comes from within us because He dwells in our spirit. God can use dreams, visions, mental pictures, other people, or angels to send us a message. However, the primary way God speaks to us is through His Word. As we read His word, the Holy Spirit gives us revelation and understanding.

The Bible is not an ordinary book, nor is it understood naturally. It's a book of revelation, a masterpiece from the Creator to His creation. The Bible is the Word of God written by men, under the inspiration of the Holy Spirit. In the Old Testament God spoke through the prophets. As New Testament believers we have a more dependable Word than mere prophecy. We have Jesus and the Holy Spirit.

The Word of God

The following Scriptures are illustrations of what God's Word is and what it does:

Matthew 4:4… It's how man lives.
Matthew 15:6… It's the force and authority.
Mark 4:20… Seed that bears fruit.
John 1:1… God Himself.
John 6:63… Spirit and life.
Ephesians 5:26… The sanctification of the church.
Ephesians 6:17… The sword of the Spirit.
Philippians 1:14… Salvation to everyone who hears it.
Colossians 3:16… God's home in us.
Titus 1:9… Trustworthy.
Hebrews 4:12… Living, active, full of power, sharp, dividing, exposing, and judging.
1 Peter 1:23… Imperishable, immortal, everlasting seed.
1 John 2:14… Causes us to be victorious over the evil one.
Revelation 19:11… Faithful and True.

The Word of God has the power to renew our minds, taking our thoughts from the natural world to the supernatural Kingdom of God. God doesn't violate His Word; He upholds His Word. God speaks, and the Word goes forth and is fruitful. It accomplishes the task to where it is sent. God's Word is impregnated with the power to produce a miracle. God can't be tempted, nor does He tempt anyone. His Word is pure. God sets parameters with His Word and establishes our boundaries. God's Word activates our faith. The Holy Spirit quickens verses and passages, giving us revelation. The unregenerate man can't comprehend the Word. It's foolishness to him because he is perishing.

I was saved in 1981 and received the baptism of the Holy Spirit. While I was attending church, someone gave a message in tongues. I heard the audible voice of God interpret the message. I was a new Christian but had no doubt it was God speaking. Every cell in my body heard God's voice. His Words were clear, and they came from my right side and over top of me. He said, "Fear not, for I am with you always, in all things." It was a very unusual experience I'll never forget. After that, I began listening for God's voice. One of the ways was to pray in tongues and ask the Holy Spirit to tell me what I'd just said.

I have used this method for thirty-seven years. I spend a lot of time praying in the Spirit and reading God's Word. Sometimes the Holy Spirit will call me into His presence. I always get a pen and paper. I keep our conversations in journals. My grandmother heard the voice of God too. She gave me prophecies from the 1950s when she and others met in homes for prayer. The Spirit of God would come over the meeting, and people would prophesy. The meetings were taped and later transcribed. I cherish these writings with much encouragement. God wants to speak to every generation. My husband, my daughter, and my grandson hear God speak to them. God wants to speak to you too.

When I was ten I became very ill with a fever and infection. Lying in bed, I had an unusual experience with a sensation on my tongue. I dismissed the event as having to do with the fever. For twenty-one years, I would continue to have the same recurrent sensation. I had no idea what it meant. I never told anyone because I thought it was so weird!

One night, shortly after being saved, it happened again. I was praying and suddenly my tongue felt strange, just like in the past. I immediately asked God to tell me what that meant. He told me I would speak His words prophetically and they would fill an entire room. For twenty-one years, God confirmed the call on my life, even though I did not know Him. Since my salvation in 1981, I have spoken His prophetic words publicly, in corporate church settings, in prayer meetings, and in praying with individuals. This book is written according to all that the Holy Spirit spoke to me. He laid out the chapters, arranged the content, and gave me the thoughts to write.

Questions

1. What does the natural man try to do? _____
    _____
    _____
    _____

2. What are some ways to purposefully hear the voice of God? _____
    _____
    _____
    _____

3. What does God desire to re-establish with us that was lost in Eden? _____
    _____
    _____

4. What is the number one hindrance to hearing the voice of God? _____
    _____
    _____

5. When we hear the voice of God, what must we do? _____

6. What is the primary way God speaks to us? _____

7. Name three things the Word of God does. _____
    _____
    _____

8. How do we renew our minds? _____

9. How can we purpose to hear the voice of God? _____
    _____
    _____
    _____

10. What has God recently spoken to you? _____
    _____
    _____
    _____

Reflections: _____
_____
_____
_____
_____
_____
_____
_____
_____
_____
_____
_____

Prayers: _____
_____
_____
_____
_____
_____
_____
_____
_____
_____
_____
_____

Additional Scripture References for Study

James 1:5-8, Jeremiah 10:23, Jeremiah 29:11-14, Psalm 14:2-3,
Deuteronomy 30:8-14, Exodus 3:1-6, Luke 18:15-17, 2 Timothy 1:7,
1 John 4:18, John 10:3-18, Psalm 46:10, Matthew 7:9 -11,
Proverbs 4:1,20, 2 Peter 1:19- 21

Operating in the Gifts of the Holy Spirit

Chapter 4 explains all nine gifts and gives practical applications for their use. Healing and miracles are manifested gifts of the Holy Spirit. When we hear the Holy Spirit and cooperate with Him, we'll flow in His gifts to heal others. The Holy Spirit demonstrates not only the power of God but also His great love and mercy towards us. The gifts are supernatural expressions of His providence and care. They are given by the Holy Spirit and vary according to the person's need. They are extraordinary in function and unique in operation. It is impossible to heal a person apart from the working of the Holy Spirit.

CHAPTER 4

Operating in the Gifts of the Holy Spirit

There are nine gifts. They are: the word of wisdom, the word of knowledge, faith, gifts of healing, working of miracles, prophecy, discerning of spirits, diverse kinds of tongues, and interpretation of tongues.

Why Are We Given the Gifts of the Holy Spirit?

When we were saved, we were sealed with the Holy Spirit. Every born-again believer bears the mark and the presence of the Holy Spirit. After receiving Christ as Lord and Savior, we follow Him in water baptism. This signifies we are dead to the old sin nature and brought up out of the water with Christ's resurrection life, a new born-again creation.

There is a second baptism separate from water baptism. It is the baptism of immersion into the power and life of the Holy Spirit. Once we are born again and receive the baptism of the Holy Spirit, we are God's vessels made ready to cooperate with the Holy Spirit. To receive the gifts of the Holy Spirit, we must be baptized in the Holy Spirit (covered in chapter 1). As humans, we are unequipped to move in the supernatural realm apart from the Holy Spirit. However, as a new creation in Christ Jesus, we are called to walk, not after the dictates of the flesh, but with power and authority in the Holy Spirit.

God has called us to preach the Gospel, destroy the works of the devil, heal the sick, raise the dead, and establish His Kingdom here on earth. There is no way we can do this apart from the gifts and life of the Holy Spirit. The apostles established the Church under the guidance, leading, and demonstration of the Holy Spirit. If they needed to allow the Holy Spirit to manifest through them, how much more do we need this same manifestation for today's Church? Both the prophet Joel and the apostle Peter preached that in the last days

God would pour out His Spirit on all flesh. The Holy Spirit continues His work in full cooperation with the will of the Father, and we are His vessels. The gifts He gives are to demonstrate the power and love of God to heal, deliver, save, and redeem.

The gifts of the Holy Spirit are distinctive and diverse. Their usage depends on the situation for which they're needed. For instance, a person who prays for someone to get well needs the gift of faith, the gifts of healings, and the workings of miracles to be in operation. Without the Holy Spirit's orchestration, His power, and His gifts, healing can't be accomplished. Apart from the manifested gifts of the Holy Spirit, healing and miracles don't occur.

Miracles don't just happen. People say, "It's a miracle." If it is a miracle, it didn't appear out of nowhere or thin air. It is a manifestation of the Holy Spirit. When something miraculous happens, we should realize that the Holy Spirit showed Himself and thank Him for the miracle. I believe many people go unhealed because the person praying, while sincere, is not operating in the power of God through the Holy Spirit. We cannot accomplish the work God gives us alone. We need the Holy Spirit. The gifts *are the manifestation* of the Holy Spirit. They come because of the infilling of the Holy Spirit through the baptism of the Holy Spirit.

Every Spirit-filled believer (those who have received the baptism of the Holy Spirit) are potential vessels for the Holy Spirit to manifest through. We are used by the Holy Spirit as we seek Him, understand our position in the Body of Christ, and walk in the power and authority Jesus gave us. The Holy Spirit is the power of God flowing through us and manifesting Himself through His gifts. He gives the gifts as He chooses.

We do not decide which gifts we receive or how the gifts will manifest. This is the operation and the orchestration of the Holy Spirit. Our part is to submit and follow His leading as we pray for the sick. God is not a formula, and we are not waiting for God to heal. He healed us two thousand years ago at Calvary's cross. Healing was provided by every lash of the whip on Jesus's back. The beating He endured provided our healing. Healing is part of the atonement along with salvation and righteousness.

We are given gifts to make the presence of God visible to those in need and establish God's Kingdom here on earth. These gifts are supernatural, not performed by human effort, but rather released by our faith in cooperation with the Holy Spirit. Believers can't effectively serve God in their own power or strength. They need the supernatural power of the Holy Spirit. The gifts come from an unseen God. While we can't see the Holy Spirit, we see His works made manifest through these gifts.

Nicodemus was a member of the Jewish High Court known as the Sanhedrin. He was a Pharisee who came to Jesus at night to learn more. Jesus gave Nicodemus an illustration of being born again through the Holy Spirit. He compared the Holy Spirit's work of new birth as being like the wind. It can be heard and the effect seen, but the wind itself is invisible.

The Holy Spirit moves and orchestrates our lives as we are being built up into the Body of Christ. Unable to see Him, we can see the powerful demonstration and effect He has on us and through us. The wind is like the movement of the Holy Spirit. We don't see the wind move across the sky, but we see the movement of things in its path. It is the effect (the manifestation) we see and not the actual wind itself. So it is with the gifts of the Holy Spirit. We don't see Him, but we see His manifestation. We see the effects of the Holy Spirit through the gifts He manifests.

Here is an example of the working of the Holy Spirit. Let's say we encounter a life issue that weighs heavily on us. It robs us of sleep and peace and fills us with worry and torment. Day and night, we carry this burden until its weight exhausts us. When we can no longer carry it, we come into God's presence and pray.

The Holy Spirit manifests Himself. The weight and the care of the burden fall off our shoulders, and we have a renewed sense of peace and hope. We come in one way and leave another. We had an encounter with the unseen Holy Spirit. We didn't see Him, but we leave with the *effect* of His having worked on our behalf.

The world doesn't know or recognize the Holy Spirit because Jesus hasn't sent Him into their lives. He operates in the world but not in the spirit of an unregenerate person. Only a born-again person encounters the presence of the Holy Spirit. Therefore, the operation and giving of gifts is only through the cooperation of a person who has accepted Christ and who has been born again.

The gifts of the Holy Spirit have been given to build the Church so that we can preach the good news of the Gospel, establishing the Kingdom of God. The Holy Spirit doesn't just reside in us. He operates in us to the extent we submit to His leading. He manifests His presence with nine separate and distinct gifts. These gifts are for the people we witness to or pray for, with the intention of showing them God's love and compassion.

The gifts are for the one *praying* to help the one *receiving*. In other words, I don't have a gift of healing and therefore heal the sick. The giver of the gift is the Holy Spirit; the receiver of the gift is the person in need. We are the conduit God uses to reach others with His love and grace. Whatever gifts the Holy Spirit confers through the believer, He confers them so He may do the work and will of the Father. No one has them merely for himself.

The gifts aren't given for show or superiority. When a person is healed, we take no credit. Our response to their healing is to glorify God and praise Him for His goodness. Having said that, I may be the *one* in need. As I pray for myself, the Holy Spirit can manifest and give me healing or revelation to my situation. I am the one praying and receiving. The Holy Spirit helps me and supplies what I need.

How Are the Gifts Dispensed?

It is important to note that a believer is not restricted to one or two gifts of the Holy Spirit. In other words, it is the Holy Spirit who manifests Himself through the gifts for a particular need. The person ministering to the one in need, if yielded to the power of the Holy Spirit, may be used in any of the nine spiritual gifts. The Holy Spirit gives the gifts as He sees fit. We don't have ownership of the gifts. They are the way in which the Holy Spirit expresses the love, power, and glory of God to the person needing help.

Many times, we wrongly believe a person is gifted and they minister in one or two particular gifts. I have flowed in all nine of the gifts of the Holy Spirit throughout my Christian walk. Also, it is possible for multiple gifts to be in operation at the same time. The key is to listen to the Holy Spirit and do what He says.

I believe the days of large healing ministry organizations in the Body of Christ are coming to a close. Not for any misuse of their work but because God is pouring out His Spirit on all flesh. I also believe God is raising up many members in the Body of Christ, teaching and equipping them to heal the sick and set the captives free. God wants to use ordinary people to touch the sick and heal them.

Many people are too sick to travel or wait for the crusade to come to their town. Healing services began in early tent ministries and rented auditoriums by the pioneers of faith like Wigglesworth, Roberts, Kuhlman, Summerall, Schambach, Hagin, Hinn, McNutt, and Copeland, to name a few. These were men and women who stepped out in radical faith, believing the Holy Spirit would do miraculous things through them to help others. They paved the way for us and showed us how to have faith for healing and miracles. Today God is moving through individuals of little renown.

Unfortunately, some believe that only the head of a ministry has the power to heal them. They won't let anyone else pray for them. Instead, they wait in line and only receive prayer from one leader. In doing this, they exercise no faith. Their faith is not in God but in the person. This is wrong doctrine. The power of God is not limited to a person...*it is not human power...it is God's power.* Jesus said to have faith in God, not in the person praying.

If we put our faith and trust in God, He will use us ordinary "unknowns" to do extraordinary things. Even Jesus did not personally lay hands on and heal everyone that was healed. He gave His disciples the authority to heal and cast out devils in His name. They went out two by two and did it with great joy and miraculous results. Every believer is a potential vessel for the Holy Spirit's use. It's not the gift of the believer; it's the gifts of the Holy Spirit in operation through the believer. In other words, the Holy Spirit manifests in the gifts through the believer for the good of a person in need.

As believers, we're not responsible for the outcome of these gifts upon another person. Our position within the Body of Christ is to pray and ask to be used by the Holy Spirit. It is a step of faith to reach out and heal the sick, but we shouldn't shrink back. As we read God's Word, our faith becomes stronger. We have fellowship with the Holy Spirit and realize that He will manifest with gifts through us for the good of another person.

> **Mark 16:17-18 (KJV)**
> **¹⁷ And these signs shall follow them that believe; In my name shall they cast out devils; they shall speak with new tongues; ¹⁸ They shall take up serpents; and if they drink any deadly thing, it shall not hurt them; they shall lay hands on the sick, and they shall recover.**

The Holy Spirit is working in us and through us. I'm not responsible to heal a person, nor am I the one who takes the accolades for the healing. My part is faith in God and submission. Another key to being used to heal the sick is to stay away from pride and remain humble, willing, and obedient. The Holy Spirit is the judge of how His purposes are best served. He chooses which gift or gifts He will operate and manifest through. It's not as we will or as we think it should be, but it's as the Spirit of God pleases.

Description and Usage of all Nine Gifts

Word of Wisdom. This is a revelation gift, giving wisdom for a situation or need. It's specific to an event, not an impartation of wisdom for all things. It comes when seeking God for explicit direction when praying for someone or something. It can also be for God's wisdom in making personal decisions and always in seeking God's will for the church or an individual.

Example: In 2015, God led us to sell our home. Through Scripture, dreams, and prophetic words, the Holy Spirit expressed wisdom in every process. He gave us wisdom to pack, list, and set the price. We also had wisdom as to who would buy the house and how to hold firm to our asking price. God gave us wisdom to purchase our current home, set a price, and close. There was not a single part of the process we did in our own wisdom. We relied on the gift of wisdom from the Holy Spirit.

As we sought the Holy Spirit, He gave wisdom to make right decisions; ones that lined up with His will and plan for our lives. We were able to close on our house one day and close on the new house the next day. We were told that was not possible, but the Holy Spirit did it. We were debt free and in our new home.

Word of Knowledge and Understanding. This is an insight gift when reading and studying God's Word. It manifests as an understanding of Scripture. The gift can also occur when praying for someone or about something. God reveals something which is hidden or secret. In healing the sick, sometimes there is an obstacle that is preventing healing. A word of knowledge and understanding is the key to success.

Example: While on a medical mission trip to Ukraine in 1996, a woman came to the clinic with severe abdominal pain. She was doubled over and crying uncontrollably. I prayed and laid my hands on her abdomen. The Holy Spirit manifested in a word of knowledge through me and said, "Ask her who she needs to forgive."

As I spoke through my interpreter, the lady told me she hated the Russian government for causing the Chernobyl release of deadly radiation. She continued to tell me they had lied to her and denied responsibility. She believed her stomach pain was the result of radiation exposure. I told her she must forgive them. I encouraged her to look to Christ for help and said, "Will you forgive them?" As I embraced her, she said, "Yes." Immediately the pain left her body and she stood up praising God. I never prayed for her to be healed. I let the Holy Spirit manifest through me with His gifts, and He did it all. That situation needed to be unlocked by something secret, something that was blocking her healing. I have experienced this many times in ministering healing. Take your time when you minister to a person. Don't be in a rush; allow the Holy Spirit time. He will do a complete work.

Example: A lady asked me to pray for healing of the skin on her forehead. She had a rash that covered her scalp and travelled down her face. When I prayed the Holy Spirit showed me the problem was the conditioner she was using. I prayed for healing, and she stopped using the conditioner. Had I not listened to the Holy Spirit, I would have prayed, but the problem would have continued. These are the situations that can cause people to believe God does not want them well, and the devil is right there to reinforce that lie.

The Gift of Faith. This gift is a supernatural ability to believe God's Word and be assured of something before it happens. It's for us to use when we pray for others, to encourage them to believe and trust God. This gift allows us to look beyond the natural realm and stand in faith until God answers. It isn't ordinary faith nor is it salvation faith. It is a gift of faith for a specific event. It is supernatural faith to look beyond what is seen and receive what is needed.

Example: My husband was gravely ill in December of 2010. The doctors believed he would not make it out of Critical Care alive. For days Jim would come in and out of consciousness. I battled a spirit of death and continued to speak life into him. On the fifth day, I was sitting alone in his hospital room. Jim had been taken to the Imaging Department for a renal biopsy and then dialysis. I began to read the Gospel of John. I was exhausted, fearful, and battle weary. I desperately needed God's peace and His Word to settle me. I read the following verses:

John 14:27 (AMP)
Peace I leave you, not as the world gives do I give to you. Let not your heart be troubled... don't be agitated, disturbed, fearful, intimidated, cowardly or unsettled.

John 16:33 (AMPCE)
I have told you these things that in Me you may have perfect peace and confidence. In the world you will have tribulation, but be of good cheer, I have overcome the world and stripped it of its power to harm you.

A supernatural faith took hold of my heart and mind. It was as though Jesus were speaking directly to me. My strength returned. I was at peace and knew Jim would live. I was confident, not in the physicians but in the Word of God. The battle was over, and nothing I saw made me doubt.

I went to the dialysis unit and spoke with Jim's nephrologist. I asked him a simple question, "Is Jim out of the woods yet?" He looked at me like I was delusional! He said, "Out of the woods? Jim is in the deepest, darkest part of the woods." You see, the gift of faith is so real it defies the natural realm. In this instance, the Word of God was more real to me than Jim's illness or the words of a physician. I wasn't in denial of my husband's grave condition, nor did the doctor's answer move me or make me upset. I knew the Holy Spirit had given me unshakable, supernatural faith to move this mountain and restore my husband to health. Nothing was going to rob me of His gift.

In the next few days, Jim continued to improve. The doctors and nurses were astounded. They even told us that they did not expect Jim to live. But he did, and he walked out of the hospital healed, to the glory of God. This kind of faith doesn't look at circumstances; it looks beyond what is seen in the natural to the miracle that's coming in the supernatural. The battle is won first in the supernatural realm then manifests in the natural realm. As long as I saw sickness and death in the natural, the fight continued; but as soon as I saw the victory in the Word of God and received it by faith, the battle was over. This supernatural gift of faith allows us to believe supernaturally. God is the giver of all good gifts. He sends them from the supernatural realm, and they manifest through the Holy Spirit to us.

Gifts of Healings: These are plural gifts, which manifest through us to heal another person without the aid of medicine or human intervention. They are plural gifts of healing because of the wide variety of sicknesses and by the way in which they manifest. They can manifest through laying hands on the sick or sending the Word of faith to the sick person.

Example: The Holy Spirit has manifested through me many times in the past thirty-seven years. As I have laid hands on people, I have witnessed healings of various acute and chronic pain and all types of diseases. These include cancer, fibromyalgia, abnormal blood counts, macular degeneration, back pain, earaches, headaches, toothaches, broken bones, and many more, as well as casting out demons of fear and torment.

Working of Miracles: This gift is supernatural and differs from healings because it is recreative. Things like growing a limb, seeing a new eye form in the socket, growing a new organ, or raising the dead. The gift takes place immediately and supersedes the natural realm. It can manifest in any situation needing immediate and divine intervention. According to the Assemblies of God website, "This can include spiritual deliverance from demonic forces, physical deliverance of God's people in ominous life-threatening situations (Acts 12:6-19), a positive change of favor in the midst of difficult circumstances, and timely provisions for human need (Matthew 14:13-21)."[7]

Example: Many years ago, my dog excitedly jumped up on my elderly grandmother and tore the skin on her hand. The gash was about two inches long. I laid hands on it and prayed. When I took my hand away the wound had completely healed over with no scab or scar.

Example: I was in Ukraine in 1996 on a medical missions trip. I was in a staging area with hundreds of people waiting to see our physicians. Sitting in one of the chairs was a woman who was very ill. I went over to pray for her. All of a sudden, she slumped over and died. There were no vital signs. I immediately sent for help. I began speaking to her and commanding her to live. In about ten minutes she sat up, look startled, and was instantly well.

The Gift of Prophecy: This gift is speaking or writing a message from God. It's for both the Church at large and individual believers. It is for strength, encouragement, and edification. It foretells the future and gives vision to the Body of Christ. The Assemblies of God website states, "Every manifestation of this gift must be weighed by other members of the congregation to see whether it is in line with Scripture."[8] The apostle Paul said of all the gifts, we should earnestly desire this one.

---

[7] "The Gifts of the Holy Spirit," web page for the Assemblies of God Church. Permission granted by the General Council of the Assemblies of God, Springfield Missouri, November 28, 2017, https://ag.org/Beliefs/Topics-Index/Gifts-of-the-Holy-Spirit.
[8] Ibid.

Example: In 1981 after I was born again and baptized with the Holy Spirit, I wanted to talk to God and have Him talk to me. My obstacle was doubt. I struggled with trust. Like many people, I was unsure if it was God speaking to me or if it was my own voice. I practiced listening and writing what I heard. I have written hundreds of conversations with God. This book is written in the prophetic voice of the Holy Spirit: His instructions, His wisdom, His words, and the Father's will. Line by line the Holy Spirit has guided me to write, edit, and publish. It's for you, to help you know and understand the call on your life with simple, practical revelations.

The Gift of the Discerning of Spirits: This gift is the ability to distinguish truth over deception, especially when it comes to the Word of God, false prophets, and demons. This is a supernatural gift to recognize and distinguish good from evil. It's a strong sense of knowing God's Word and discerning doctrinal error through wrong interpretation of Scripture and secular influence. Both can overtake the church and someone's ministry. It is also given for discerning biblical truth versus New Age religion. Many secular and humanistic doctrines have surfaced, and sadly some in church leadership have fallen into deception and ruin. This gift is necessary to lead the Church in truth and away from error, especially as the Lord's return draws near. Deliverance of demons needs the gift of discerning spirits also.

Example: The Holy Spirit can manifest this gift through visions and words. I remember one morning while working in Orlando. I took the back stairs up to CICU. As I pressed the automatic door to open, I immediately saw above the door what looked like black moss hanging down. I saw this in the spirit, not in the natural. The Holy Spirit instantly revealed there were demonic spirits of death and sorrow that operated in this unit. This portion of the unit contained only four beds, but it was used for the sickest patients. Death was the usual outcome for anyone in this area. I took authority over the demons and commanded them to leave and never return. When I exited the unit, the demons were gone.

This gift has manifested in my life many times over the years by showing me strongholds of the enemy when I pray for people. This gift is key to deliverance. Witchcraft, occult, drugs, alcohol, and sexual sins are open doors for demonic entrance. As this gift is in operation, the Holy Spirit will show areas where people need to renounce the devil and ask God's forgiveness. Jesus cast out demons many times in healing the sick.

The Gift of Divers (Different) Kinds of Tongues: There is much confusion about this gift because there is little understanding. Some churches don't allow speaking in tongues. The Bible tells us that tongues should not be forbidden. As stated on the Assemblies of God website, "Tongues are Spirit-directed languages from heaven. They are unknown, even to the one who speaks them. When people speak in tongues the Holy Spirit anoints them and they are spiritually edified (strengthened and built up) through union with

God. This edification happens without one ever knowing what is said. Such edification is experienced individually by the one who prays in tongues."[9]

To help clarify some of the confusion, it can be said there are two administrations of the gift. One is for corporate use in Christian gatherings, and the other is for the believer's private prayer language. Both are tongues, but they each have a different function and purpose.

Corporate Tongues: The Holy Spirit gave the gift of tongues on the Day of Pentecost. One hundred and twenty disciples of Jesus had gathered in the Upper Room. They spoke in unknown tongues (languages). Many people in Jerusalem were from other countries, and all spoke a different dialect. As the disciples spoke in tongues, everyone in the city heard the Gospel of Jesus Christ in their own native language (tongue). Because of this miraculous act, three thousand people were saved in one day, and the Church in Jerusalem was born. Therefore, *divers kinds of tongues* is a sign for unbelievers, and it can't be understood without interpretation.

Currently, there are over seven thousand known languages. The Bible has been translated and reproduced all over the world in the different languages. Different kinds of tongues are still given by the Holy Spirit and used in church meetings to equip the people in worship, praise, exhortation, instruction, and correction. This gift always needs an interpretation of the message.

Example: I have spoken in corporate settings and in my prayer language; both are tongues. Some have asked, "How will I know if I'm to pray in tongues in a corporate setting?" First, pray and ask the Holy Spirit to manifest through you to give you boldness to speak. Then wait and have faith that He will. The Holy Spirit is gentle and not rude. He will not give you a message while someone else is speaking. There is a time to speak up. It usually follows praise and worship when the congregation is waiting to hear a message from the Holy Spirit.

Example: In 1996, my husband and I were accepted to be part of a large medical outreach to Ukraine. This was to be our first medical missions trip. As the time for departure got close, my husband found out that his job demanded he stay behind. We met with our pastor and prayed. It became obvious this was *not* an attack from the enemy but the will of God. I did not want to go alone so far away. I gave God all sorts of excuses as to why I could not go. Finally, after several days and sleepless nights, I surrendered, telling God yes.

That night during the church service, I wept at the altar. I kept saying one word in tongues, *Toc, Toc, Toc,* over and over again. A year later God called me back to Ukraine without

---

[9] "The Gifts of the Holy Spirit," web page for the Assemblies of God Church. Permission granted by the General Council of the Assemblies of God, Springfield Missouri, November 28, 2017, https://ag.org/Beliefs/Topics-Index/Gifts-of-the-Holy-Spirit.

Jim. This time I was in western Ukraine where the language is not Russian but Ukrainian. (Most of Ukraine speaks Russian.) As I listened to the dialogue, I heard the word "toc" for the first time. I was told it meant "yes" in Ukrainian. The night I had wept at the altar, saying the word "Toc," I was speaking in tongues. In the Ukrainian dialect, I was saying "yes" to the will of God; "yes" to trusting God to go alone where He was calling.

My "yes" became a nonprofit medical organization, started by us, lasting eighteen years. My "yes" was ten years of orphan support and eight years of drug and alcohol rehab provision in Ukraine. My "yes" was nine trips into Ukraine. We helped thousands of people hear the Gospel and see the goodness of God. Do I believe in tongues? *Toc,* I do.

Personal Prayer Language Tongues: The Bible refers to this as praying in the Holy Ghost or praying in the Spirit. It is for private and personal prayer. It's prayer that comes from our spirit through the Holy Spirit to the Father. It's tongues and sounds like the gift of tongues. We are to pray at all times, staying alert. Praying in the Holy Spirit (tongues) also strengthens and builds up our faith.

Example: Whenever I'm going through a challenging event, I pray in the Holy Spirit. I pray until I get a release of faith and a real sense God has the problem and is working everything out for my good. So this *building up* the apostle Paul speaks of is a shoring up, a strengthening of our faith so we can be overcomers.

When we're praying prayers in agreement with the Holy Spirit, praying isn't laborious. It's restful, easing our worry and fears. There is a confidence in the power of God when we pray in the Spirit. We're able to rest, knowing the Holy Spirit's in charge. He knows what we need to pray in every situation. As we trust Him, the way is made clear to us.

You can pray in your prayer language for hours whenever or wherever. You control your prayer language. You decide when to pray and when to stop. You are the vocal cords, tongue, and lips for the Holy Spirit to speak through. So you can pray while driving, working, relaxing, grocery shopping, anywhere, anytime. When we don't know what to pray or how to pray, we have the help of the Holy Spirit. He is the Truth, Wisdom, Teacher, Intercessor, Helper, and the One who stands by us.

After praying in tongues, ask the Holy Spirit to give you the interpretation. It's the best part because we understand with our mind what we prayed in our spirit. He will give you revelation knowledge and will supply answers you couldn't receive on your own. This is another reason the devil fights so hard against receiving this gift. He is afraid of what will happen when we pray in tongues as part of our daily Christian walk.

The more you read, meditate on the Word of God, and pray in tongues, the stronger your faith becomes. Set aside time daily to pray in the Holy Spirit. Start a journal, and you will be amazed at what the Holy Spirit prays through you. As you sit quietly in His presence, ask the Holy Spirit to interpret your tongues and write it down. Make a habit of this, and soon you will recognize the voice of God speaking to you.

Remember, this prayer language is just one of the gifts God wants to give you through the baptism in His Spirit. In asking for the baptism, you are availing yourself to receive His gifts, pray strategic prayers, perform miracles, advance God's Kingdom, and allow the Holy Spirit to further cultivate the fruit of righteousness in your life.

The Gift of the Interpretation of Tongues: This gift works in unison with the gift of divers (different) kinds of tongues in a corporate setting because there's a need for an interpretation. A message is given in tongues, and the Holy Spirit gives the interpretation (not the translation) of the meaning. There must be someone who can interpret if the gift of tongues is in operation.

Example: Tongues without interpretation is not understood by the mind. Therefore, the Holy Spirit gives interpretation for our understanding and edification. In a corporate setting, there must always be interpretation. However, in private prayer language, tongues may or may not be interpreted. It's interpreted if we will take the time to ask the Holy Spirit for the interpretation.

If I'm praying in tongues and I hear the Holy Spirit give me a thought or understanding about the matter, I immediately come into agreement with Him. This is very important. How can we line up or have faith if we don't know what the Holy Spirit is saying through us? Wait and seek the interpretation. This will enrich your prayer life with amazing results.

We are built up and edified when we pray in the Spirit. If I feel as though I am slipping out of faith into doubt, I pray in the Spirit and I'm restored. The Holy Spirit knows the heart of God and the will of God. He alone is able to intercede for us as we pray in Him.

Questions

1. Why are believers used in the gifts from the Holy Spirit? _____
    _____
    _____

2. Why did Jesus compare the Holy Spirit and being born again to "the wind"? _____
    _____
    _____
    _____

3. Who does the Holy Spirit move in full cooperation with? _____

4. Why can't the world recognize the Holy Spirit? _____
    _____
    _____

5. Which of the nine gifts did the apostle Paul say is the best gift? _____

6. Why did he say it was the best gift? _____
    _____
    _____

7. How does the gift of faith differ from faith in God? _____
    _____
    _____

8. What is the difference between the gifts of healings and the working of miracles?
    _____
    _____
    _____

9. Why is the gift of the discerning of spirits important? _____
    _____
    _____

10. Why does a message in tongues need interpretation? _____
    _____
    _____

Reflections: _____

_____

_____

_____

_____

_____

_____

_____

_____

_____

_____

_____

_____

_____

Prayers: _____

_____

_____

_____

_____

_____

_____

_____

_____

_____

_____

_____

_____

Additional Scripture References for Study

1 Corinthians 12:1-31, John 3:8, Acts 2:1-11, 1 Corinthians 14:1-40,
Ephesians 6:18, Jude 1:20, Romans 8:27, 1 Corinthians 2:1-16, Hebrews 2:3-4

Righteousness

Chapter 5 adds another foundational truth to our victory in Christ. We must understand that our righteousness before God is not our own righteousness. It's God's righteousness given to us, by faith, in the Lord Jesus Christ. There are no *good works* we can do to justify ourselves before an Almighty Righteous Judge. Jesus is the perfect sacrifice. He shed His blood for the remission of our sins. As we apply our faith to what Jesus did on the cross and His resurrection from the dead, we are made righteous in Him. His righteousness gives us access to the presence of God. As New Testament believers we are now in a grace covenant with God through faith in Jesus. Our faith in Him has great reward. We've been made righteous in God's sight through Jesus.

CHAPTER 5

Righteousness

Understanding the provision made available to us through Christ's death, coupled with our faith in Him, is key to living a victorious life. It's also a key to healing the sick. While power and authority belong to us in Christ, a far greater gift has been placed *in* us. The gift is righteousness, being in right standing with God, and our sin debt paid.

At the cross, our sins were placed *in* Jesus. When we receive Him as Lord, His righteousness is placed *in* us. Our faith has great reward, not just in heaven's eternity, but also here on earth. As such, it's the area in our lives most attacked by Satan. If we lose faith, we lose our inheritance. If we stop believing in what Jesus did, thinking it's what we can do, we become self-righteous and forfeit His righteousness. It's not in the efforts of the flesh that salvation and righteousness are attained. It is faith and faith alone in what Jesus did.

Righteousness is the great exchange of Calvary, our sins for God's righteousness. It allows us to come before God in a perfect, sinless state. There's no other way for mankind to attain righteousness apart from the shed blood of Jesus. No one goes to the Father except through His Son. Not only are we forgiven, but we are also made righteous to the standard of God Himself.

Once we fully grasp this gift, our walk with Jesus changes from being sin conscious to righteousness conscious. We're not victorious if we're dwelling on our sin, shame, faults, and failures. Jesus took all those things to the cross and made us, through faith in Him, righteous before God. No one can achieve this state of perfection on his own because each of us has disobeyed God and broken His commandments. Before we accepted Christ as our Savior, we were separated from God because of sin. We were separated not because of love but because of justice. God is love but He is also the Righteous Judge.

In the Old Testament, righteousness was obtained by keeping the law. When man sinned the law was broken and restitution was required. When Adam and Eve sinned, God made a blood sacrifice to cover their offense. He covered their shame and guilt in the skins of animals. A life for a life is what God required. As long as people made blood sacrifices and kept the law, they were made righteous in the sight of God through their works.

In the New Testament, righteousness still requires a blood sacrifice. Instead of animals, Jesus was killed in our place. He's the perfect lamb, slain for our sins. By His death and resurrection, He has purchased and redeemed us back to the Father. It was the shedding of His blood, once for all, which puts us in right standing with God the Father.

Under the old covenant law, when Israel sinned, they took a perfect unblemished lamb to the priest for a sacrifice. Before the sacrifice, the priest inspected the lamb. If it met the conditions of perfection, the priest laid hands on the lamb and transferred the man's sins to the animal. Then the priest sacrificed the lamb.

Notice who is inspected; *it's the lamb*, not the man. The man is guilty and brings a sacrifice to pay for his sins. There's no point in looking at the guilty man. He can't free himself from the consequences of his sins. The lamb is inspected because the lamb is going to take on the sins of the man and be sacrificed. The innocent lamb is exchanged for the sins of the man. It's the lamb that must meet the requirements of God and be accepted for the forgiveness of sins. When John looked up and saw Jesus coming to be baptized, he said, "Behold the Lamb of God who takes away the sin of the world. "

> **John 1:29 (KJV)**
> **The next day John seeth Jesus coming unto him, and saith, Behold the Lamb of God, which taketh away the sin of the world.**

John not only acknowledged Jesus as Messiah, but he also spoke out the words of grace and redemption that would come through Jesus as our sacrifice. Just as the priest inspected the lamb, God the Father inspected His Son, declaring Him acceptable, the only perfect sacrifice.

God's not looking at us to be the perfect lamb. He looked at Himself and declared Himself perfect. When the enemy condemns you and me for our sins, we can say to him exactly what John said, "Behold the Lamb who takes away the sin of the world." The enemy may remind us of our sins, but he can't condemn us. We can say with blessed assurance, "Yes, I am a sinner, but behold the Lamb of God. Look at my perfect lamb, the Lord Jesus Christ who took my sins away."

Romans 8:1-2 (KJV)
There is therefore now no condemnation to them which are in Christ Jesus, who walk not after the flesh, but after the Spirit. ² For the law of the Spirit of life in Christ Jesus hath made me free from the law of sin and death.

To be in right standing with God, we must surrender our lives to Jesus and receive Him as our Lord and Savior. He did the perfect work on the cross. The only work God requires today is to believe in His Son and accept His sacrifice for our sins. Merely acknowledging His death is not enough. We must, by faith, surrender our lives to Jesus. By faith, we are covered in the blood of Jesus and made righteous in His righteousness.

Works, sacrifices, or being a good person doesn't put us in right standing with God. There must be an acceptance of God's requirement for righteousness. It's acknowledging our need for a Savior, asking forgiveness for our sins, and inviting Jesus to be Lord of our lives. It's faith in Him that puts us in right standing with God. All other means for right standing with God are unacceptable. There is only one way to the Father; it's through the Son.

As New Testament believers we have a more excellent sacrifice; we have the perfect Lamb of God, who takes away the sin of the world. We come before God in what Jesus did, not in what we do. Our righteousness is as filthy rags compared to the standard of righteousness God demands. Our rags are covered in the filth of hypocrisy, self-righteousness, and pride. The garments He offers through His Son are the only fitting attire to wear before the King. Righteousness is the moral perfection required by God to enter heaven. Nothing but the blood of Jesus pays the price. How do we get in and stay in right standing with God? *By faith in Jesus.* This is a prophetic word given to me by the Holy Spirit regarding righteousness:

> *When I spoke to Moses and said, "I AM THAT I AM," I made a declaration of My supremacy and My power. I would go on through the years and reveal My identity through My names. The children of Israel had to be taught that I was above all other gods, all authority, all powerful, all creative, all-sufficient, all healing, all love, all provision, all righteous, all knowing, ever present, all peace, transcendent, creator, holy, healer, restorer, immutable, sovereign, almighty, master, Lord, wisdom, faithful, gracious, benevolent, judge, capable of wrath, merciful, and just. Moses could never have understood My name, and so I was to him, I AM.*

> *When I came to Abraham, I took him from worshipping false gods and the making of idols to becoming the father of many nations. Through him and his offspring, I established My identity. The descendants of Abraham, Isaac, Jacob, and all others had to be taught who I was to them. Experiences became their teacher. Whatever*

they needed, I AM was their answer. Each time I would reveal Myself, a manifestation of who I AM became clearer to them.

Each of My names describes who I AM. So it is to this day. I still reveal Myself through My name, the same Name that is revealed in My Word. As you experience the trials and impossibilities of this life, I am made known to you more clearly through these experiences. I am the God of the Old Testament and the God of the New Testament. After the fall of Adam and Eve, mankind lost fellowship with Me due to disobedience and sin. In that loss of fellowship, they had no one to teach them. No one searched after Me; no one knew that they even needed My presence.

I created man to worship Me, in love and union with Me. When I warned them that sin would bring death, it also brought darkness and ignorance. Union with Me was cut off. A few men, Enoch and Noah, found favor with Me. With Noah, I made a covenant with him and with all living creatures, but it was not until I made a covenant with Myself to Abraham that revelation of I AM would begin.

One of the most prominent attributes of God is righteousness, which is synonymous with justice. God is the righteous judge and therefore can't overlook sin. Like a human judge, upholding the law and showing no partiality, there are consequences and penalties for breaking laws. God's Kingdom laws guide us in right decisions. They are instituted for our good and for our protection. They are the boundaries that shore up our borders, setting a framework of limits and freedoms.

Before Adam and Eve disobeyed God, they were sinless, righteous, and in fellowship with God. He gave them provision, work, and only one command. It was their boundary line. Once they broke the commandment, they broke fellowship with God. When they sinned, God's justice was enacted. Their disobedience had a severe penalty, and the penalty was death. Sin had consequences, just as our sin and the breaking of God's commandments have consequences today.

God hasn't changed. He's still the righteous judge. Not only was there death, but expulsion from the garden, and from the very presence of God. They lost their *righteous status* when they disobeyed Him. Sin produces guilt and guilt produces shame. Shame brings blame, and blame drives us further from God. He created us to fellowship with Him, placing within us a longing for worship and communication. Sin breaks that communication. With communication cut off, worship becomes perverted and turns to idolatry.

Adam and Eve were the first generation of mankind. Twenty generations later Abraham was born. Up until the time of Abraham, only two men, Enoch and Noah, found favor with God. God's communication with man was very limited. Noah obeyed God and built the ark. His obedience saved him, his family, and all the animals. God made a covenant with Noah and set a rainbow in the sky, promising to never again destroy the earth by a flood.

Abraham obeyed God by leaving his country, kinsmen, and his father. He set out, in faith, to a place unknown to him. Abraham believed God and obeyed Him. It was counted to him as righteousness. God rewarded Abraham's obedience and promised to make him the father of many nations. Today we refer to Abraham as father Abraham because it was through his faith in God that the nation of Israel came to exist. He did no works to become righteous. He had faith, and he obeyed God.

> **Romans 4:16-25 (AMP)**
> [16] Therefore, [inheriting] the promise depends entirely on faith [that is, confident trust in the unseen God], in order that *it may be given* as an act of grace [His unmerited favor and mercy], so that the promise will be [legally] guaranteed to all the descendants [of Abraham]—not only for those [Jewish believers] who keep the Law, but also for those [Gentile believers] who share the faith of Abraham, who is the [spiritual] father of us all— [17] (as it is written [in Scripture], "I HAVE MADE YOU A FATHER OF MANY NATIONS") in the sight of Him in whom he believed, that is, God who gives life to the dead and calls into being that which does not exist. 18 In hope against hope Abraham believed that he would become a father of many nations, as he had been promised [by God]: "So [numberless] SHALL YOUR DESCENDANTS BE." [19] Without becoming weak in faith he considered his own body, now as good as dead [for producing children] since he was about a hundred years old, and [he considered] the deadness of Sarah's womb. [20] But he did not doubt *or* waver in unbelief concerning the promise of God, but he grew strong *and* empowered by faith, giving glory to God, [21] being fully convinced that God had the power to do what He had promised. [22] Therefore his faith WAS CREDITED TO HIM AS RIGHTEOUSNESS (right standing with God). [23] Now not for his sake alone was it written that it was credited to him, [24] but for our sake also—to whom righteousness will be credited, as those who believe in Him who raised Jesus our Lord from the dead— [25] who was betrayed *and* crucified because of our sins, and was raised [from the dead] because of our justification [our acquittal—absolving us of all sin before God].

Three Biblical Timetables

To properly interpret Scripture, we need to understand God's timeline and the covenant requirements. From Genesis to Revelation, the Bible is compiled of three separate timelines. If we don't discern the timeline correctly, we mistake the Word of God. As New Testament believers, we need to stay in grace and not the law.

First, the period of time before the law. It lasted from Adam to the time of Moses. It was a type of grace where men like Noah, Enoch, and Abraham found favor with God through faith and obedience. Both Noah and Abraham made blood sacrifices to honor God.

Second, the period of time when the law was given. God instituted the law through Moses. It lasted up to the time of Jesus's death. Man's sins were forgiven if he kept the demands of the law. Righteousness was obtained through blood sacrifices. When man sinned, he became unrighteous and had to atone for the sins. It was a serious charge, one that bore the death penalty for disobedience. Once God instituted the law through Moses, all things became subject to the law. Both of these periods are known as the Old Testament or old covenant.

Third, the period of time from the resurrection of Jesus to His return. Today, believers live in grace, called the new covenant. Faith in Jesus, His death on the cross, and resurrection puts us in right standing with God. By faith in Christ, God imputes righteousness to us because we've believed and received His Son.

The law of Moses could never remove man's sin. The sacrifice of bulls, goats, and sheep were only a covering for man's offense to God. Why is this important? There are several reasons, but for this text, the importance lies in the authority and righteousness of the New Testament believer. Right standing with God isn't achieved through good works and sacrifices as it was in the Old Testament. Our works are as filthy rags compared to the righteousness and holiness of God. If we try to come before God in our righteousness we put ourselves under the curse of the Old Testament law.

We have no basis or foundation for authority and righteousness when we try to produce it ourselves. It's only as we receive Christ and put our faith in what He's done that the Father receives us into His holy presence. Once there, the Kingdom of God belongs to us. We have Kingdom responsibilities and Kingdom rights. Under grace, righteousness is imputed to every believer through Jesus Christ.

From Adam to Moses, there was no law. Righteousness was found in faith and obedience. After the institution of the law, righteousness was found by keeping all the law and offering animal sacrifices. Jesus came and fulfilled all the requirements of the law and now the Church lives under the grace of Jesus's righteousness. Our very sin nature keeps us from acting in the righteousness and the perfection God requires. The law was never intended to make man righteous, but instead was a mirror showing his pitiable state and desperate need for a Savior.

Why Was the Law Given?

Three months after the children of Israel left Egypt, while camped in the wilderness of Mount Sinai, God gave Moses a message for the people. Coming down from the mountain, Moses gathered them together. God reminded them of His faithfulness and goodness. He promised to make them a treasure above all other people if they would obey all His commandments. Instead of humbly asking for God's help, their reply revealed the condition of their hearts, exposing their own *self-righteousness*.

They answered Moses and told him to go tell God they could do all He commanded. Based on their response, God had to show an unrighteous people what was needed to obey all He commanded. God called Moses to the mountain, and the stone tablets were written. God continued to give Moses many more laws written in the old covenant.

The law was rigid, perfect in form and structure but lacking the ability to change the heart. It would serve as a tutor and trainer until the time Jesus came. Atonement for lawlessness kept man from death. It covered man's sins but never made him righteous. Just as the children of Israel had been slaves to Pharaoh, living a life of servitude, now they lived a life of servitude to the constraints of the law. Sin thrives under the law because the strength of sin is the law. The law points out every fault and is the perfect environment for sin consciousness.

Every time a law was broken, a sacrifice had to be made. The law was a constant reminder of their sins and failures to meet the expectation of being righteous. God was paving the way for a redeemer, a savior. He Himself would come and deliver the world from the law and from the penalty of sin. The law was unbending, unforgiving, and uncaring. It had high standards and strict punishment. Anyone breaking it either died or made restitution, depending on the severity of the transgression.

God's standard of righteousness was unattainable. The law's purpose was to show man his sinfulness and need for forgiveness. The weakness of the law could only point out sin, not remove it. The law had no power to change men's hearts and actions. It only focused on works through imposed rules. It actually promoted sin through self-righteousness. The law made man more aware of his sinfulness. Mercy and grace didn't factor into the demands of restitution.

To summarize, God gave the law knowing it couldn't be kept. Man had to understand his sinful ways before a righteous judge. God knew there was a better way, and in His perfect plan, at the right time in history, Jesus came to earth. Just as Moses had come to deliver the children of Israel, so Jesus came to deliver all mankind. Not just to save the Jew, but to save all creation.

Grace Replaces the Law

Grace and truth came through Jesus Christ. He wouldn't do away with the law but would fulfill it and all its requirements, even to His death on a cross. Love would win, and God's perfect plan for His creation would be complete. His longing for us, coupled with His perfect love and desire to be with us, drove Him to an act of extreme obedience to save us.

Today the Church is in a grace covenant with God. Jesus shed His blood and died in our place. He paid the ransom for our sinfulness. Just like Abraham, our faith in Jesus credits us with the righteousness of God. Without Jesus, there's no way for man to stand before a holy God and be the righteousness His justice requires.

God desired to become broken to deliver us from our brokenness. Sin had separated and blinded us to His love and mercy. Jesus came and showed us God the Father. Jesus was the initiator of the new covenant, a covenant of grace, life, and love. Grace is the favor God shows us. Grace is God choosing to bless us rather than condemn us. Grace doesn't do away with justice, but it's the fulfillment and product of justice. Grace is the person of Jesus Christ, giving us what we couldn't obtain for ourselves.

No amount of law keeping could purchase our right standing with God. Salvation is the gift that ushers in righteousness. Righteousness takes us to the throne room of God where we can be in His presence once again. God initiated our redemption. He came to rescue us and redeem us. The righteousness God requires comes through faith in Jesus. It's a gift to whosoever will believe.

Jesus's blood was poured out as a sacrifice for our sins because the law demanded payment for our disobedience. No one is justified through works. Christ purchased our redemption and freedom. Now we are justified through the righteousness of His Son. When God looks at the believer, He sees His Son. He sees the nail prints in Jesus's hands and His blood on the mercy seat of heaven.

Today some in the Body of Christ have been deceived by the devil in the area of righteousness. They don't understand the meaning of the word *impute*. God does not *impart* righteousness to us as though it's an external gifting of grace. He *imputes* righteousness to us. Our sins were imputed on Christ. He (Jesus) who knew no sin became sin that we would become the righteousness of God in Him. Just as our sins were imputed or put upon Jesus, now His righteousness is imputed to us. We who knew sin and were sin have become righteous because Jesus exchanged our sins for His righteousness.

When we fail to understand the great exchange at Calvary, we move to our own works for justification and righteousness. This promotes the keeping of the law, the very thing Jesus redeemed us from. The focus is on works, prayers, penance, sacraments, fasts, the traditions of men, and Old Testament laws. These things place people back under the law, making the Gospel of no effect. Righteousness is the result of our faith in Christ. That is why the devil works so hard to get us into unbelief.

Many people I pray with have a sense of rejection or a belief that God is not pleased with them. The devil sows these lies with the goal of relegating the child of God from a position of authority and power to that of an unforgiven sinner. He is a liar! No one can earn Christ's righteousness because it must be received as imputation from Christ to us. Works do not make us closer to God. They put us back under the law. If the law is the guide, then all the law must be kept. The law says you must pay...but grace says *I have paid in full.*

Our righteousness comes from our faith in Jesus. There at Calvary, in the agony of His suffering and subsequent death, a great exchange happened. God Himself came down from heaven, leaving its glory and splendor. No palace or luxurious furnishings; just a humble, smelly shed with animals. He was wrapped in swaddling clothes, like those used to wrap His body after death. He was laid in a wooden feeding trough, where animals ate. He would lie down again on a wooden cross, where He, who was the finest wheat, was crushed and killed. He was the bread, the manna that came down from heaven to die a painful, humiliating death for us.

The wood of the cross, like the wood of the trough, represented our life, nourishment, and salvation from death. Being God, He took on our fragile form and redeemed us back with His own perfect blood. His obedience to the cross canceled the disobedience of Adam and Eve. Our sins were not only forgiven, but our debt was also paid. In that great exchange, He took our unrighteousness and gave us His righteousness. He took our sickness and disease and carried them in His own body and we are healed. God Himself bore our sins and grief, and in exchange gave us eternal life, righteousness, and forgiveness.

To receive from God, to be in God's presence, to fulfill God's plan for salvation, we must have faith in Jesus. We can't come to God asking for something based on our works or our goodness. With that attitude, our prayers go unanswered. We must approach God just as Israel did, with a sacrifice. Instead of our sacrifice being an animal, our sacrifice is Jesus, the Son of God. Behold the Lamb, who takes away the sin of the world. Christ is the end of the law, having fulfilled all the law, we move *in Him* to grace.

I believe the reason we are tempted to return to *works* is because we don't really understand what being made righteous means. We need to look beyond our flesh and our emotions and look to our spirit. It's our spirit that was dead and then made alive to Christ when we became born again. Our righteousness, which comes through the redemption Jesus provided on the cross, dwells in us through faith. Righteousness is not in the flesh or in the soulish realm of thoughts. It's in the place where the full Godhead dwells. That place is our spirit.

We have been made new, recreated in our spirit—not in our flesh or in our minds. For example, the day I accepted Christ I became a new creation. My outward appearance didn't change. My hair color, my frame, and my age all stayed the same. I was thirty-one in the natural, but I was a newborn baby in my spirit. The change in me came from the inside out, not from the outside in. My desires changed, I wanted to know God's Word, and the old sin habits fell away. I wanted to be good and please God. The change wasn't in my body; it was in my spirit.

Our bodies are perishable. Our minds (souls) are where we think and feel. Our minds must constantly be renewed in God's Word. *Our spirits* are where the new nature of God infuses and makes us one with Him. God makes our dead spirit alive when we accept His Son as the gift of our salvation. When we say yes to Jesus and invite Him to live in us, God puts the Spirit of His Son in us. *God dwells in our spirit*. When the Father looks at us, He sees His Son. We no longer fall short of the glory of God because the glory of God is Christ, and Christ dwells in us.

We stand before God in what Jesus has done. Jesus has taken our sins and given us His righteousness. God doesn't change His mind. He won't violate or go against His Word. Those who haven't made Jesus their Lord and Savior are spiritually dead. Everyone born has been born spiritually dead because of the sin of Adam and Eve. They have no true spiritual life even though they may profess some false religion. No other religion can bring the dead to life—only Jesus Christ and His power. He alone is the Resurrection and the Life.

Jesus told Nicodemus he had to be born again. He thought Jesus was speaking of natural birth, but Jesus was speaking of the spirit, not the flesh. Unless a person is born again, they cannot see the Kingdom of God. The message of sin and salvation in Christ is nonsense to them. They are dead! To those who are dead and perishing, this Gospel is foolishness to their carnal minds.

Feelings and the Enemy's Deception

Satan has been stripped of all power. His weapons are deception and trickery. His war is waged first in our minds and then in our flesh. God created us with powerful emotions, which have been seduced by the god of this world. Feelings and emotions are influenced by our senses: what we see, what we hear, and what we feel. The devil is skilled at imagery and deception. He wages war in our minds, using emotions and thoughts of failure and death. The enemy is the tempter. If sin is committed, he'll condemn with guilt, unworthiness, and lies. After that, it's a natural response to believe we've offended God.

Some even believe they lose their salvation. This is a lie from the devil, part of the deception. If we can understand the enemy's tactics and know who we are in Christ, we can defeat him and destroy his works. Our mind forms our thoughts. Therefore, God has instructed us to renew our minds. Our minds must move beyond the physical senses and concentrate and meditate on truth, which is God's Word. Our minds aren't made perfect in righteousness; they need to be renewed in God's Word. It's our spirit that's made perfect in Christ and in His righteousness.

Only a person who is born again and meditating on God's Word will have a mind controlled by a righteous spirit. The Word is what makes our spirit stronger; it's our spiritual food. God tells us not to be led by our flesh but to be led by our born-again spirit. Satan can't attack our spirit. He can only attack our mind and flesh. Why would Satan want to attack our mind? When an individual receives Jesus Christ and is born again, he instantly becomes a new creation in Christ and an *adversary of the devil*. The devil hates God. He wages war at God and all God's creation.

Satan has always wanted to destroy man. Before we were born again, we were his servant, yielding to his will and committing sin. The moment a person receives Christ, spiritual warfare is declared. The believer is a threat to his kingdom of darkness and his demonic forces. Our weapons are God's Word and our obedience to Him. Jesus defeated Satan in the wilderness by quoting Scripture. The Word of God is our sword for this battle. Therefore, we must spend time studying the Word, meditating, believing, using and doing what the Word of God instructs. The Word is life and spirit. It has the power to produce miracles and to grow faith.

Religion and Self-Righteousness

Where there is no law, there is no transgression. For instance, if I'm driving on the German autobahn going ninety miles an hour, I'm not breaking the speed limit because there's no speed limit. There's no law governing how fast I can go. Therefore, any high speed I choose is lawful! However, where there are laws there is also the penalty for breaking them.

The Old Testament law magnified sin. It brought condemnation, guilt, and demanded payment when broken. The law pointed out man's sins by drawing attention to everyone's actions. Sinning might have been a private event, but it became public repentance. Animals were chosen, carried to the priest, inspected, and sacrificed. Sin abounded because it was the focus of the law. In fact, sin was the strength of the law. The problem with the law was no one could keep it. So there was sin, guilt, the sacrifice of works, forgiveness, and the cycle continued.

Sin thrived in this environment. As more laws were enacted, the potential for sin and guilt grew. Instead of man drawing closer to God, the law actually drove man away from God. The law was a religion of dos, don'ts, and works. It was instituted by God and was perfect. Perfect in condemnation and perfect in pointing to man's inability to obtain right standing before God. It was perfect to cover sins, and it was perfect in showing man their need for a Savior.

With Christ, we have a more glorious covenant. A new and everlasting covenant. This covenant not only covers our sins, but also makes us sinless before God. It justifies us before God because it hinges on Jesus's works and not our works. The righteousness that Jesus provides is free of guilt and condemnation. By His grace, we are free from punishment. We are put back into fellowship with God. In that magnificent union with our Creator, we find salvation, healing, deliverance, purpose, and provision for the good life God has planned.

Religion and self-righteousness are fruits of legalism. They rob us of true freedom and acceptance in God. Jesus warned His disciples about self-righteousness when He addressed the works of the Pharisees. What did He mean when He told the disciples their righteousness must be more than that of the religious Jews of the day? The leaven He spoke of represented sin, and their sin was the most odious kind. It was pride and self-righteousness, all the things the law promoted.

The reason the religious Jews were so offended by Jesus was because He offered grace and forgiveness apart from religious works. They were jealous to the point of murder. While they kept the law, prostitutes, tax collectors, lepers, and others they deemed unfit were being set free, healed, forgiven, and loved, all apart from having to do anything. Jesus was preparing the way for a radical, new approach to God. What had been works would soon become faith in the One who would fulfill all the law in perfection.

Jesus preached faith in God and love for one another. He showed mercy and gave grace. He moved the people because He spoke to their hearts and not to their faults. No human could have ever fulfilled the law—only God Himself. No amount of rules, sacrifices, and works could make a person righteous and sinless.

The religious crowd hated Jesus because they prided themselves on their appearance of superiority. Not only was mercy withheld, but obstacles were also placed in the path of those seeking God. The Pharisees controlled the people and yet were powerless in their legalism. They couldn't understand why Jesus hung out with such sinful people. If that weren't bad enough, His disciples were illiterate, unsavory, and uneducated. The more grace Jesus gave to sinners, the more incensed the Pharisees and religious leaders became. Jesus asked nothing of the sinner but to repent and believe in Him, the same thing He asks of sinners today.

Religion based on works promotes self-righteousness. The religious Jews were no different from religious Jews or Gentiles today. Self-denial and works are a way of glorifying oneself rather than giving all the glory and honor to Jesus Christ. It's also a way to compare ourselves with others. We reason that we're not as good as some but not as bad as others, as if that were God's measuring stick.

Looking around, we justify our actions based on the actions of others. The world is not God's standard of righteousness. God is God's standard of righteousness. Our only justification is to completely place our faith and trust in Jesus. This acknowledgment of what He did negates our own self-righteousness, giving full credit and honor to Jesus. Our righteousness isn't based on works but rather on faith in the works Christ did.

God takes great offense in self-righteousness because it says Jesus, His only begotten Son, who died for us, isn't enough. It says we have to add to what Jesus did. If we could make ourselves righteous, Jesus could have stayed in heaven and off Calvary's cross. But God, so rich in mercy and love, died for us. He paid the demand and the death penalty with His life. We must accept His death as God's righteous requirements and move away from self-righteousness.

The Robe of Righteousness

Jesus taught a parable to His followers, which is an illustration of law versus grace. The story is a contrast between dependence on oneself and dependence on Jesus. One day a king gave a wedding feast for his son and invited many people. Some refused the invitation and killed the messengers. The king sent out another invitation to find as many as possible to come to the feast. The hall was filled with good people and bad people alike.

When the king came to see his guests, he found a man inappropriately dressed and he had him thrown out. His attire was the reason for his dismissal. The man was dressed; he wasn't naked or in rags. However, the king had provided something of necessity, something of beauty, something expensive, and something required—wedding clothes! The man ignored the king's provision and instead came in his own clothes. What was the message of the parable?

Those and only those, who put on Christ, who live by faith in Him, have put on the wedding garments provided by the King. No one wearing their own good works can enter into the wedding feast; only those in proper attire. Jesus is our covering, our provision.

Our trust in Him is the only clothing the King will accept. The King calls many to the wedding feast. You and I are given an invitation.

Although many are called, the majority come dressed in their own clothes. They don't accept the King's coverings, and because of that, few are chosen to enter into the wedding feast. The clean linen spoken of in Revelation 19:8 refers to the righteousness of the saints. Our real holiness and sanctification are provided in Christ. He has made us righteous. He is our covering. The Lamb of God died in our place and has given us His robe of righteousness.

When we heal the sick, it's God's righteousness in us that answers their prayer for healing. It's not our righteousness that causes a person to be healed. We've been made righteous. In other words, we are the righteous vessel the Holy Spirit uses to manifest Himself. The gifts are in operation because of the baptism of the Holy Spirit. As we lay hands on the sick and release our faith in God's power, His virtue and His resurrection life flow through us to them. There are no good works we can do to manipulate God into healing someone. It's not by our goodness; it's by His righteousness given to us when we first believed in Him. Our faith in His righteousness and power are all we need to heal the sick.

All sickness is a form of death. Disease involves a part of the body or mind that is suffering. That specific portion of the body is not healthy and left untreated, the disease can spread and the person will die. When healing the sick, we are releasing our faith in the power of God and allowing His life to flow into the area of need. We speak to the sickness and disease, commanding it to leave the person's body. Then we speak life where disease once had hold and forbid the sickness to return. By doing this, we come against the plan of the enemy to steal, kill, and destroy. Jesus came that we might have life and have it in abundance. We speak the Word of God to the sickness, with authority as believers and with righteousness given to us by Jesus.

Questions

1. Define the word righteousness. _____
   _____

2. According to the prophecy, how did God reveal Himself to the children of Israel?
   _____
   _____

3. After the fall of Adam and Eve and before Moses instituted the law, how did God communicate with man?_____
   _____
   _____

4. Why can't the law cleanse us of unrighteousness?_____
   _____
   _____

5. Why wasn't the perfect law perfect?_____
   _____
   _____

6. What replaced the law and how did that happen?_____
   _____
   _____

7. Why are so many Christians confused about righteousness?_____
   _____
   _____
   _____

8. What part of us is dying? _____ What part of us needs renewing? _____
   What part of us is righteous? _____

9. Why can't our own works save us?_____
   _____
   _____

10. Who did Jesus come to save? _____
    _____
    _____

Reflections: _____

_____

_____

_____

_____

_____

_____

_____

_____

_____

_____

_____

Prayers: _____

_____

_____

_____

_____

_____

_____

_____

_____

_____

_____

_____

Additional Scripture References for Study

Galatians 3:6, Philippians 3:8-9, Galatians 2:16-21, Romans 4:5, 13-15,
James 2:10, John 1:12, Romans 3:10-26, Galatians 3:10-14, 24-25,
Romans 5:18-21, Isaiah 64:6, Ephesians 2:12-20, Ephesians 4:22-24,
Romans 8:10, 1 Corinthians 1:18, Proverbs 4:23, Proverbs 23:7,
Romans 12:2, Luke 5:21, 2 Corinthians 3:9, 2 Corinthians 5:21, Romans 4:5, 10:3-4,
Luke 7:37-50, Luke 5:32, Matthew 5:19-20, Matthew 16:6, Matthew 22:1-14,
Isaiah 61:10, Exodus 19:1-19, Mark 6:56, Philippians 3:7-10

God's Will for Healing

Chapter 6 begins with a prophetic word regarding God's will for healing. God is not only able to heal, but He's also willing to heal all who come to Him in faith. There is no sickness, disease, or diagnosis too difficult for Jesus to heal. Very little faith, the size of the tiniest seed, is required. More faith is not necessary. The key is faith without doubt or unbelief. Jesus healed countless people while here on earth. His atonement on the cross provided our healing. Our bodies are proof that God desires to heal us. He created each system to work in cooperation to maintain health. Take the human heart for instance. The average heart beats 115,220 times in a 24-hour period, based on eighty beats per minute. In one year, that same heart beats 42,048,000 times. By the time the person is eighty, his heart will have beat 3,363,840,000 times. No machine can match the human heart. God has also given knowledge and ability to the medical profession with advancements in technology to help keep us in perfect health. If God has done all this, He's certainly willing for us to be healed and to stay healthy.

CHAPTER 6

God's Will for Healing

The following is a prophecy given to me in 2016 regarding God's will for healing:

When you heal the sick, you destroy the works of the devil. You bring My Kingdom to that person. You bring My love, My deliverance, and My power to them. ALL healing is a manifestation of My Spirit. It is a gift I give to the person; it is a display of My glory. The enemy uses trickery and deception. Some of the ways the enemy works against healing are division, strife, anger, jealousy, envy, and manifesting false symptoms. He also uses distraction, procrastination, depression, lethargy, lies, accusations, pride, arrogance, and self-congratulatory attitudes. Spiritual warfare is necessary to defeat his tactics.

God Wants You Well

Jesus lived thirty-three years on earth. The last three were in public ministry. He came to destroy the works of the devil, to bring salvation to mankind, and to show us God's love and mercy. He was God in the flesh. He taught us how to live in relationship with God and one another and how to obtain salvation through believing in Him. He healed the sick everywhere He went. He cast out devils and performed mighty miracles. The Gospels record miracle after miracle through the eyes of His disciples. Everyone who came to Him for help was changed, both physically and spiritually. Jesus never rejected anyone, nor will He reject you.

God has not changed. He remains the same. He doesn't heal some and not others. If He healed all who came to Him two thousand years ago, He will heal all who come to Him today. If He brought us the way of salvation then, it remains the way of salvation today.

If He stripped the devil of all authority, then the devil has no authority now. God is a God of order, not chaos. He's not one way today and another way tomorrow.

In the last chapter of Mark's gospel, Jesus gave His followers a final set of instructions. They were to preach, heal, and deliver. They were to proclaim His name and His Gospel throughout the world. Surely those final words were very important. He warned them against their unbelief and hardness of heart. If there are two things that prevent us from seeing the sick healed, it is *unbelief and hardness of heart.* They are discussed further in this chapter.

To heal the sick, we must settle this heart issue of whether or not God wants to heal them. It's a crucial key to seeing the miraculous. If we vacillate between is it or isn't it His will to heal, then we are double-minded and receive nothing from God. There's no faith in being double-minded because one moment we believe and the next moment we doubt. If we pray for the sick and aren't sure God wants them well, we do great harm to the person's faith.

Praying for the sick is not hoping they get well; it's knowing they will. We must be confident in God and His will to heal. God allows us to bring any situation to Him, even doubt. When we are in doubt, we can ask God for wisdom and He will give it freely. It's imperative we seek God, asking Him to reveal the truth. However, it's unacceptable to be the vessel of healing if we don't believe it's God's will to heal.

Some denominations have taken a passive position, believing "if God wills it, it will happen." That attitude requires no faith on the part of the person praying or the person receiving. It provides an easy way out in the event nothing happens. Even more heretical, it puts the blame on God or the person if healing doesn't manifest. Many a harmful blow has been dealt to people in a prayer line when they are told their faith wasn't enough to manifest healing. Never have the attitude "if God wills it." Healing is God's will. Not only does His Word confirm His will, but He has also made the human body with every system in place to promote healing.

Our bodies are designed to heal themselves and to maintain health. The medical profession with all its modern-day advancements has come about because it's God's will to heal. To be God's vessel takes boldness and stepping out in faith. The further your faith is stretched, the more results you will see. Timidity won't win the battle. Faith takes courage and determination. Passivity requires nothing and produces nothing.

What if I pray and nothing happens, or what if I pray and the person dies? Even if the person doesn't immediately manifest healing, it doesn't mean God's Word didn't activate and produce a healing. You had faith, you were obedient to pray, and the results were up to God. I've seen instant healings, healing that took place within the hour, and gradual healings that took a little longer. Our responsibility is to pray the prayer of faith, not only believing, but also *expecting* the Holy Spirit to manifest. Scripture bears out testimony to the fact that God extending the life of dying people and raised the dead. Pray, believe, and expect the same mercy and grace to be evident again.

God Has Already Done His Part

Jesus is not healing people today. He healed us two thousand years ago at Calvary's cross when He suffered and took our sins. He took our sins and gave us His righteousness. He took our diseases and provided healing. The cross is the great place of exchange. We have healing waiting for us. It has already been provided. The same faith that saved is the same faith that heals. We're not waiting for God to heal us—He is waiting for us to receive it. God sent His Word, and He has already healed us. The Word of God is Jesus.

When the Word is spoken, it is like a seed being sent forth. The seed is sown into the soil of the person's heart where it produces fruit. The Word of God, the Bible, is not a book of ordinary words, nor a series of stories and events. Jesus said His words are Spirit and life. His Word accomplishes where it's sent and doesn't return void. Healing and miracles are in the Word. Satan is the thief. He comes to steal, kill, and destroy. He doesn't want your house, your car, or your money. He wants the Word, which is sown in your heart. His war is against the Word of God, sown and taking root in the heart, producing faith, and receiving healing and miracles.

The Word is waiting for us to respond. Faith comes by hearing the Word of God. Healing and miracles belong to us, by faith, just as salvation belongs to us. If I'm saved, then I'm also healed. If salvation is mine in the name of Jesus, then healing is mine in the name of Jesus. We mistake the job of getting healed as something we need to earn, when in fact, it is something we believe and receive because Jesus earned it for us. God's goodness and grace provided our healing at Calvary, but we must use our faith to receive the provision.

We Have Been Given Authority Over Sickness and Disease

We have been given the power to heal the sick through the presence of the Holy Spirit within us. From the study in chapter 2, "Authority of the Believer," we know God has sent us out to preach the Gospel and heal the sick.

The Kingdom of God Is Here

Eternal life began the moment we were born again. The Godhead infused Himself within our spirit, and we are one with Him. We were dead and became alive, born again, born from above. Eternity isn't in the by-and-by; it's now. The Kingdom of God is here inside us. We are the temple of the Holy Spirit. Many times, Jesus said the Kingdom of God is here. If the Kingdom is here, the King is here, and if the King is here, He has all power and authority in heaven and on earth. How can sickness and disease stay?

Jesus taught His disciples to pray asking for God's Kingdom to come and for the Father's will to be done here, like it's being done in heaven; that the Kingdom of God would reign in heaven and on earth at the same time. This is happening today all over the world as Christians obey and seek God's will for their lives. Earth is to mirror heaven. When Jesus returns, He will reign on the earth for a thousand years.

Is there cancer in heaven? Is there any ailment in heaven? No. Then it has no place here on earth either. Jesus commissioned His disciples to go and heal the sick. He gave them His authority and power. We have the same command with the same provision. They were successful, and so are we. Jesus told them to go and heal the sick. He didn't tell them to go to the sick, find out what's wrong with them, get some medical help, and then tell God what the doctor said. He told them to go and heal the sick.

This may sound elementary and repetitive, but I want to draw attention to the ways the devil sets traps for us. Satan wants to engage us in conversation. He did it with Eve. The more she talked, the more he deceived her. God had given a simple command, but Satan turned it into a debate. This is still his tactic today. He wants to draw us into a long conversation; to talk with lots of people, research the Internet for hours, tell God what the sickness is, what the symptoms are, and what the doctor's report says. Once that happens, our focus is lost.

The command is to heal the sick, one simple command, but we exchange the assignment for the deception. God knows far more about the sickness and disease than we could ever convey. It has not caught Him off guard. In fact, God is so on guard that He healed us two thousand years ago. God is way ahead of us!

We are commanded to heal the sick—to speak to the sickness, the symptoms, and the doctors' reports. Speak the Word of God in faith. Healing is a settled matter with God. It's already been purchased and is waiting for us to receive. There needs to be an understanding that our healing waits for us. We are not waiting for God to heal us—He is waiting for us to receive it. We are asking God to do what He has already done.

Here is an example of what I mean. A child asks for a bike for Christmas. He goes to his parents and leaves no doubt as to what he wants. The child is very specific about size, color, and make. Christmas day comes, and the parents decide to surprise the child. They hide the bike in the garage. The child inquires about the bike and the parents tell him to go to the garage. The child continues telling the parents what he wants, why he wants it, and asks why he didn't get it. The parent continues time and time again to tell the child to go to the garage. This is exactly what we do. We keep asking God for something that is already ours.

Finally, after much frustration, tears, and maybe temper tantrums, the child is exhausted. The parent takes the child's hand and leads him to the garage. There is the bike. It's exactly what he wanted: the right color, the right size, and the right model. The bike was there all along. It had been provided weeks ago by loving parents who wanted to give the child his heart's desire. They went to great lengths and expense to secure the bike, even putting it together while the child slept and hiding it until Christmas morning.

Healing is the same as the bike. Our loving parent provided it two thousand years ago. It waits in the realm of the spirit for us to go and get it. It's ours, totally custom made. All we have to do is receive it. So why do we keep asking God to heal us when healing has already been purchased? I believe it's because we don't know how to go into the spirit realm and bring what we need to the physical world. Faith and belief in God's Word are the way we receive what is already ours.

Do you know why cancer is so hard to heal? It's because we've given it so much power through fear and funding! We have given it a color, we have given it a month, and we have walked for it, run for it, and made clothing for it. You might argue and say, "Oh no, Millie, we're raising money for a cure and for awareness." Cancer doesn't need any more awareness. People are frightened at just the thought of the biopsy report coming back with the word cancer!

I won't even address all the billions of dollars spent on building pavilions and centers because cancer is big money and even bigger merchandising. Why don't we stop feeding it with attention, growing it with money, empowering it with fear, believing it is too difficult for God to heal, and start cursing it as the thing from hell it is? If people would get off the Internet, stop reading and believing all the statistics, all the death and hopelessness, and turn to the Word of God, they would find peace and life.

Those of you who know Jim and me know we've both received a diagnosis of cancer. We no longer have it. We wouldn't allow it to find a place in us. Never call a diagnosis *my* as in *my* heart attack, *my* cancer, *my* allergies, *my* whatever, unless you want to throw out the welcome mat and invite it in. My beloved brother died of esophageal cancer in 2013 because he believed God allowed him to have it and didn't want him to be healed. He died a Christian with a profession of faith in Christ. He loved Jesus and his church, but he died because he believed the lie rather than the truth that he was already healed.

Death and life are in the power of the tongue. Stop speaking death! Many people speak death and don't realize it. Speaking death means saying words that bring illness to us or keep us sick. They block healing because they align with death and disease. An example of this would be saying things like, "Every year about this time, I get sick from the pollen. It's terrible and I seem to get worse every year." Or this one, "You know, my uncle died at sixty and my father died at sixty. I guess that's when I'll die too." Sometimes we say things when we are frustrated like, "This just drives me crazy," or "I hate such and such." Words may sound benign but they're powerful. They give the enemy an open door because they express a predicted outcome.

We tend to believe what we say, especially if we say it often enough. The longer we say something negative, the stronger it becomes. The best antidote I've found in my personal life is to repent and ask God to cleanse me of the sin of speaking death rather than speaking life. Our words either make a covenant with what the Word of God says, or they make a covenant with what the enemy is doing. Sickness leaves as we exercise authority over it. We've been given power, authority, and dominion for the purpose of establishing the Kingdom of God here on earth. If God spoke all creation into being, then we must also speak.

All things created were accomplished by voice activation. God spoke and there was creation. Jesus spoke, and people were healed, Peter walked on water, the harlot avoided stoning, a fig tree withered, a paralytic walked, lepers were cleansed, blind eyes were opened, the deaf heard, possessed people were set free, and soldiers fell back in the garden of Gethsemane. When God speaks, power is released. When we speak to the illness and release our faith in God's power, His power is released and the person is healed.

Resist the Devil and Flow in the Anointing

Satan uses stolen authority through deception. He's trespassing where he has no legal right. Jesus stripped him of all power and authority. He's subject to the name of Jesus, and he's subject to us when we speak in the name of Jesus. Much of sickness is demonic, especially mental sickness, because the mind is the battlefield. Many of the miracles Jesus performed involved casting out devils. Jesus called them unclean spirits or spirits of infirmity. He commanded them to be silent and to come out. He healed many who were oppressed by the devil. The devil is a defeated foe that refuses to give up.

You don't need more anointing or a greater anointing to heal the sick. I don't need a car that goes faster if I don't know how to drive. We should apply knowledge to wisdom, doing things in the manner the Holy Spirit requires. I believe as we have a more effective understanding of our position in Christ we'll see greater miracles. There's no need for more anointing because it's not our power healing the sick. When we realize it's not us, we will see more manifestation and more miracles. We have Jesus, the One who is anointed. He resides in our spirits, through the Holy Spirit.

The anointing flows through the Holy Spirit, manifesting in His gifts. We don't need a greater anointing because we already have the greatest anointing. We have the person, we have His name, and His authority to use His anointing. Jesus doesn't anoint us with a special anointing so some of us can heal others. The Holy Spirit gives the gifts of healings and the workings of miracles. It's not our anointing, it's His anointing, His gifts, and His power. We have a far superior anointing through Jesus. His anointing flows through us, as His vessel, to those in need. All we need is faith in Him!

Acting on Your Faith

Faith requires action. After I have prayed and released faith for healing, I immediately ask the person to do something they couldn't previously do. I ask them to move, stretch, or bend, and I ask if the pain is better or gone. If full healing has not manifested, I speak again, commanding the sickness to leave. The enemy's resistant to leave, but he's the intruder. Evict him firmly with authority and be bold. He's the profane thing that has set himself against God. The only authority he has is the authority you give him.

When my dog is barking unnecessarily, I don't timidly say, in a low voice, "Please stop barking." No! I speak with authority and boldness, "Quiet, no barking!" It's effective. He knows I mean business and the barking stops. The devil is like the barking dog. Speak with the authority Jesus has given you! I say these words:

> *Devil, you have no right here. I rebuke you and command you to get your hands off. You have no authority, but I have all authority in the name of Jesus. You are defeated. Jesus has all power and authority, and I use His name against you. Go and never return to this person again. I cancel your assignment. I curse the plan you have to steal, kill, and destroy, and I release the life and power of Jesus flowing through me to you. Be made whole right now. In Jesus's name. Amen.*

Again, I ask people to do something they previously couldn't. In almost every instance they've been able to move in a way they couldn't before. Faith must be exercised!

Hebrews 11:1 (KJV)
Now faith is the substance of things hoped for, the evidence of things not seen.

Substance is something that's real. When I think of substance, I think of something hearty, solid, not flimsy, and having a real existence. Evidence is tangible proof and verification, like a sales receipt or proof of something that did or didn't take place. We sometimes incorrectly think of faith as something ethereal, without form, and indescribable. However, look at the meaning given in Hebrews. Faith is substance and its evidence. In other words, it's real, and it's now. It's indisputable, able to be confirmed, and without argument. Faith is power—not our power, but God's power.

Dispelling the Myths

From time to time, I encounter people who believe a lie perpetrated by the devil. There are a lot of lies people believe, things that block healing. If we are to be successful in stirring their faith to receive, we'll need to dispel the myths. Here are some of the more common deceptions people believe. One of the things I say before I lay hands on someone is, "Do you believe God gave you this sickness? And do you believe God wants you well?" I need to hear, no and yes. If not, I look for the myth, the lie that they have believed, and I address it according to God's Word.

Myth #1: God allowed this disease to come on me, or God gave me this sickness to teach me a lesson.

Answer: Jesus came to destroy the works of the devil. He healed all who were sick. He is the same yesterday, today, and tomorrow. He doesn't change. A loving father doesn't make his children sick. He makes provision for his sick children. It's a lie from the devil to accuse God of putting sickness on His children. We live in a fallen world, with fallen human beings. We have polluted the environment, we have hurt our own bodies, and hurt one another. God is not the author of sickness and death.

Myth #2: God is punishing me for my sins, which is why I am sick.

Answer: God punished His Son in our place. Jesus was beaten, bruised, and crucified for our sins. There's only one perfect sacrifice, Jesus. God's not angry with you. He poured all His anger and wrath out on Jesus. Jesus took God's anger. He stood in our place and received our punishment. Jesus is God, the second person of the Trinity. God Himself took the punishment for the entire world. He is satisfied with His sacrifice.

Myth #3: It must be God's will for me to be sick.

Answer: If people really believe it is God's will for them to be sick, they should stop trying to get well! In trying to get well, they are striving to be out of God's will. This is irrational thinking, twisted, and perverted because it is a lie from the devil perpetrated in the mind of a person, with one intention: to destroy the person's faith and hope, with the eventual desired outcome of blaming God and losing faith in Him.

The devil is the destroyer, he's the liar, and he brings about death and destruction. He plants seeds of doubt and lies, blaming God and accusing Him of intentionally putting sickness on people and then convincing them it's God's will. The devil is a master manipulator and a deceiver. A righteous, holy, loving God, who sent His only Son to die for our transgressions, never wills us harm. God is not the destroyer. Jesus is the giver of life. Every good and perfect gift comes from the Father above.

If God wanted us to be sick, He wouldn't have sent Jesus to heal us. In turn, Jesus wouldn't have sent out His disciples to heal the sick. There would never be any cures, wellness, healings, and miracles. Doubt arises when a person becomes ill, prays to be healed, and nothing manifests in the natural. The longer healing is delayed, the more time the enemy feeds fear, doubt, and unbelief. The devil's goal is to defeat your faith. The longer a person lives with chronic illness and pain, the weaker they become in that area of faith. This is exactly why we need the Body of Christ to minister deliverance, healing, and restoration to one another. According to Pastor Bill Johnson, "How can God choose not to heal someone when He already purchased their healing? Was His blood enough for all sin, or just certain sins? Were the stripes He bore only for certain illnesses, or certain seasons of time? When He bore stripes in His body He made a payment for our miracle. He already decided to heal. You can't decide not to buy something after you've already bought it."[10]

Myth #4: God won't give me more than I can handle.

Answer: This is a popular phrase people say when they encounter a big trial, especially sickness and disease. The theology is when they can no longer bear the burden, God will relent and bring help. This is wrong thinking and wrong biblical interpretation. The devil loves to twist and pervert the Word of God. He did it in the garden of Eden, he did it to Jesus in the wilderness, and he is still doing it today. Their interpretation implies God is up in heaven and has decided to give them a huge problem. Maybe it's a financial need, problems with a marriage, a life that's out of control, a bad report from the doctor, all things that are part of this earthly life. These things come under the category of being *a curse*.

Jesus hung on a cross and became *the curse* so we might be free from the curse and inherit every spiritual blessing. God isn't sitting up in heaven with a scale, a clock, and the names of everyone here on earth, figuring out just how much and how long each one needs to suffer. Nor is He adding up how much penance and works are offered up to Him before

---

[10] Bill Johnson Ministries, "Is it always God's will to heal someone?" http://bjm.org/qa/is-it-always-gods-will-to-heal-someone/.

He intervenes. Those are exactly the thoughts the devil gives in the situation. Here is the Scripture that is so often misinterpreted:

> **1 Corinthians 10:13 (AMP)**
> **No temptation [regardless of its source] has overtaken *or* enticed you that is not common to human experience [nor is any temptation unusual or beyond human resistance]; but God is faithful [to His word—He is compassionate and trustworthy], and He will not let you be tempted beyond your ability [to resist], but along with the temptation He [has in the past and is now and] will [always] provide the way out as well, so that you will be able to endure it [without yielding, and will overcome temptation with joy].**

All of us are tempted. It's our commonality with one another. The temptation to sin is the subject matter in this verse. Paul was speaking to the church at Corinth about sexual sins and the temptation of adultery and fornication. Corinth was "sin city," and the sins were creeping into the early Church there. Some were committing sexual sins, acting just like the unrighteous. God wasn't giving the Corinthian church a test. Sin abounds everywhere, and we're all tempted. Of particular note in this passage: notice where God is and what He is doing. He is not far off. He is not up in heaven adding problems to their lives! He is right there with them (and us) providing an escape, providing strength to not be overcome with the temptation to sin.

Is God tempting us? No, He's with us, providing what we need so we won't sin and making sure we overcome the temptation victoriously *with joy.* This Scripture text has been grossly misquoted to mean that God is giving us something really big, but He won't make it too big because He knows what we can bear. It's a lie from the devil, a twisting of God's Word and His character. God is love, full of mercy and grace. He will not only heal us, but He will also help us when we are tempted to commit sin by providing strength and grace to resist.

God punished His Son in our place. Jesus paid for our sins. We can't pay for them. There are no works we can do to make restitution. Only the blood of Jesus pays the debt. The atonement of Christ on the cross made all provision for every need we have or ever will have. Jesus is here; the Kingdom of God is within us; He's ready to run to our cry and relieve us. God doesn't give us sickness, disease, poverty, or problems. God is the giver of life, of love, of peace, and assurance. It doesn't make us holy to suffer alone (stick it out, do enough time, pay for our sins). It makes us unaware that Jesus will run to our cry, relieve us immediately, and give us joyful victory.

Hebrews 2:18 (AMPCE)
For because He Himself [in His humanity] has suffered in being tempted (tested and tried), He is able [immediately] to run to the cry of (assist, relieve) those who are being tempted *and* tested *and* tried [and who therefore are being exposed to suffering].

God doesn't give us the burdens we bear. The truth is, He bears our burdens daily. This fallen world gives us problems, the devil who is the god of this world gives us problems, we give them to ourselves, and others give them to us. It's not God who gives them. Sometimes a sickness or disease has been present for a long time in the person you are ministering to. That person has learned to manage the disease, tolerate the pain, given up on total healing, and resigned himself to live with it. This myth also needs to be routed out. This mind-set is a lie from the enemy and a stumbling block to receiving total healing. Minister to the person and come against a demonic stronghold.

Myth #5: Jesus did not heal everyone who came to Him.

Answer: Jesus never refused to heal anyone. In fact, there are many Scriptures attesting to Jesus healing all who came to Him. There's not one single instance of someone coming to Jesus for healing and leaving sick and diseased. Even the man with doubt confessed his unbelief and Jesus healed him. People quote Matthew 13:54-58 and say Jesus didn't heal everyone. However, careful study of this text shows Jesus was in His hometown of Nazareth. He grew up there. People of the town knew His mother, brothers, and sisters. Their familiarity with Jesus caused them to miss His deity. Jesus was willing to heal them, but their unbelief prevented the miracles. Jesus did heal some in His hometown, but He didn't perform *many* mighty miracles. That's not the same as refusing to heal someone who came to Him by faith for healing.

Myth #6: God heals in His own time.

Answer: Jesus has already provided for your healing. The moment you reach out in faith and receive the promise, you are healed. God is not withholding healing for a certain time in your life. Why would He? Saying that God heals in His own time requires no faith and therefore nothing happens. People who have this notion of God healing in the "by-and-by" are being deceived. Jesus never healed anyone in the "by-and-by." Jesus healed them at the moment He released His faith in His Father.

Miracles are instantaneous manifestations of the Holy Spirit. They are one of the nine gifts of the Holy Spirit. Healings are also instantaneous acts of the Holy Spirit. Healings differ from miracles. Healings usually occur a short time after the manifestation of the Holy Spirit. This is the time when people often lose their healing because they are not standing in faith. When nothing happens in the physical realm, the natural mind, aided by the devil, surmises that a healing did not take place. They agree with the thoughts of their own mind and the enemy convinces them that God did not do anything for them.

When healing manifests, then the natural man says that God healed in His own time. That is not true. The moment you released faith, you received what Jesus died to give you. Healing was always waiting for you to receive it by faith. Christ's atonement at Calvary provided your healing. Every lash of the whip was for you and me. There is no "by-and-by" with God. Today is the day of salvation. He who has ears, let him hear.

Questions

1. Why is it important to settle the matter of healing and God's will?_____
    _____
    _____

2. What's our responsibility when we pray for the sick? _____
    _____
    _____

3. Is Jesus still healing people today? _____

4. Why is the Word of God important to receiving healing?_____
    _____
    _____

5. Besides faith, what allows me to heal the sick? _____
    _____
    _____

6. What two things are in the power of the tongue?_____
    _____
    _____

7. What two things does Satan use to block healing? _____
    _____
    _____

8. Besides anger and strife, how does Satan work against healing?_____
    _____
    _____

9. What does Hebrews 11 say faith is? _____
    _____
    _____

10. How does the enemy convince people that God doesn't want them well? _____
    _____
    _____

Reflections: _____

_____

_____

_____

_____

_____

_____

_____

_____

_____

_____

Prayers: _____

_____

_____

_____

_____

_____

_____

_____

_____

_____

_____

Additional Scripture References for Study

3 John 1:2, Matthew 17:20, Matthew 7:11, 8:16, and 9:12, Psalm 41:3-10,
Psalm 103:3, 147:3 and 107:20, Isaiah 53:5 and 61:1, Jeremiah 30:17, John 21:25,
Luke 4:18, 2 Corinthians 1:21, 1 John 2:27, James 2:18-20, Hebrews 11:1,
Hebrews 2:18, Hebrews 4:15, Mark 16:14-20

Fasting and Prayer in Preparation

Chapter 7 prepares us to be used by God. Soldiers train and prepare themselves to carry out their commander's orders. Fasting and prayer are ways we train and prepare. By shutting out the flesh's desire to rule, we give ourselves a better opportunity to hear the Holy Spirit more clearly. Prayer is essential. Jesus drew away from the noise and needs of the people to be alone with His Father. Revelations come as we fast and pray in the Spirit. God gives over battle strategies and directions, making our efforts more successful. Fasting is one way to keep the flesh in subjection to the Holy Spirit.

CHAPTER 7

Fasting and Prayer in Preparation

Does God command fasting in the New Testament? Fasting was an old covenant law first mentioned in the book of Leviticus. The purpose of fasting was for penitence, affliction, and humility. If a person didn't fast, they weren't included in the sacrifice, which meant their sins weren't forgiven. Once a year, Israel put on sackcloth and ashes. It was the Day of Atonement, Yom Kippur, ordained as a feast by God. Its purpose was to demonstrate Israel's true repentance of sin. Sackcloth was another form of showing humility and being made uncomfortable. Without a fast there was no forgiveness of sins and the unrepentant person was cut off from their people.

As New Testament believers our sins are forgiven, not by works of the law but by the sacrifice Jesus made for us on the cross. Our sacrifice is the slain Lamb of God. Our forgiveness comes by faith in Christ and His finished work on the cross. We no longer keep an annual fast, wear sackcloth, and sprinkle ashes on our head to show humility. Our being made uncomfortable should be the constant reminder of His death for us, not the wearing of scratchy clothes. Jesus fulfilled the law and preached a message of grace, not works. In turn, we are to trust Him and live a life of faith in Him. Jesus didn't speak of works and fasting but rather of repentance and belief in Him. He addressed feasting on Him, rather than fasting from food.

In John's gospel, Jesus told His followers He was the true Bread of Life. If they wanted eternal life, they had to *eat* His flesh and *drink* His blood. Some religions have taken this to mean communion, but that is a false interpretation of the Word. Communion commemorates the Passover Supper, which we call the Lord's Supper or the Last Supper. Jesus told us to take the cup and the bread and *remember* His death until He returns. It is an act of remembrance and memorial of His death, not a doctrine of transubstantiation.

When Jesus spoke of eating His flesh and drinking His blood, many who followed Him departed because the teaching was offensive and unbearable. They failed to understand parables like the vine and the branches. He wasn't speaking of a literal cannibalism, but of abiding in Him with His life flowing through them. This new life, this abiding in Him, happens when we are born again. The sin nature is dead, and our born-again spirit depends on Jesus as our necessity for life itself.

They also failed to understand there would no longer be the requirement of animal sacrifices, sackcloth, and ashes to find forgiveness. Instead they would follow Jesus and have fellowship with Him and His Father. Those who follow Jesus must abide continually in Him by grace and not works. As the branch continually abides in the vine and receives life from the vine, we receive our life from the body of Jesus Himself.

The only work required to enter the Kingdom of heaven is to believe in Jesus, to believe God sent Him, and hold tightly to Him. From this relationship and dependence, all the things we do are in His strength, His provision, and His direction. The emphasis is off us and fully on Jesus. We're here to build His Kingdom, not our kingdom. It's important we, as new covenant believers, stay in grace and in the shadow of the cross rather than in the law and the shadow of death.

What Did Jesus Say About Fasting?

Jesus entered His ministry immediately after John baptized Him. Led by the Holy Spirit into the wilderness, He fasted forty days. Is there any record that His disciples had to do the same? No, on the contrary, the Bible only records three people who ever fasted forty days. They were Moses, Elijah, and Jesus. Matthew, Mark, and Luke's gospels all give an account of what Jesus said regarding fasting:

> **Matthew 9:9-17 (AMP)**
> **9 As Jesus went on from there, He saw a man named Matthew (Levi) sitting in the tax collector's booth; and He said to him, "Follow Me [as My disciple, accepting Me as your Master and Teacher and walking the same path of life that I walk]." And Matthew got up and followed Him. 10 Then as Jesus was reclining *at the table* in *Matthew's* house, many tax collectors and sinners [including non-observant Jews] came and ate with Him and His disciples. 11 When the Pharisees saw this, they asked His disciples, "Why does your Master eat with tax collectors and sinners?" 12 But when Jesus heard *this*, He said, "Those who are healthy have no need for a physician, but [only] those who are sick. 13 Go and learn what this [Scripture] means: 'I DESIRE COMPASSION [for those in distress], AND NOT [animal] SACRIFICE,' for I did not come to call [to repentance] the**

[self-proclaimed] righteous [who see no need to change], but sinners [those who recognize their sin and actively seek forgiveness]." ¹⁴ Then the disciples of John [the Baptist] came to Jesus, asking, "Why do we and the Pharisees often fast [as a religious exercise], but Your disciples do not fast?" ¹⁵ And Jesus replied to them, "Can the guests of the bridegroom mourn while the bridegroom is with them? The days will come when the bridegroom is taken away from them, and then they will fast. ¹⁶ But no one puts a piece of unshrunk (new) cloth on an old garment; for the patch pulls away from the garment, and a worse tear results. ¹⁷ Nor is new wine put into old wineskins [that have lost their elasticity]; otherwise the wineskins burst, and the [fermenting] wine spills and the wineskins are ruined. But new wine is put into fresh wineskins, so both are preserved."

In this passage of Scripture, Jesus addresses two groups of people regarding eating, food, fasting, and mercy: the Pharisees and John's disciples. Both groups are questioning Jesus about the law and fasting. Noteworthy, Jesus doesn't use this occasion to strengthen the demands of the law. Instead, He introduces a new law, *the law of grace*. This grace will be the framework and scaffolding for the entire age of the New Testament Church. Jesus introduces the real heart of God.

In verse 12, Jesus spoke of the need for grace. He came for the sinner, not for the self-righteous. The Pharisees were self-proclaimed, self-righteous hypocrites who rejected Jesus. They paraded publicly, fasting and praying, drawing attention to their acts. They considered themselves above Jesus. While they loathed His message, they could not deny His miracles. They had no compassion or need to repent. Rightly so, Jesus did not come to save them or any other self-righteous person.

In verse 14, Jesus answers the question directly from the standpoint of grace, not legalism. There was coming a time when the disciples would fast and mourn. Their mourning quickly turned to joy when Jesus appeared to them after His resurrection. Today, we're not called to fast and mourn as the Israelites did. Our Bridegroom lives with us. We aren't alone or forsaken. We live continually in Christ and fellowship with Him. We are one with Jesus.

In verse 17, Jesus uses a parable about wine to illustrate law versus grace. He refers to old wine (Old Testament) and new wine (New Testament). Jesus's first miracle was turning water into wine at the wedding feast of Cana. He finished His ministry at the Passover Supper by saying the wine symbolized His blood, the blood of a new and better covenant. In Revelation, believers will sit at the wedding supper of the Lamb where He will drink the cup once again. Why does Jesus use the parable of the wineskins in this conversation? What is the symbolism of the wineskins?

The parable of the wine and wineskins illustrates the old covenant *law* and the new covenant *grace*. Law and grace cannot reside together. Jesus contrasts new wine to old wine, new covenant to old covenant. The wineskins are the containers or vessels holding the wine. New wineskins refer to all believers who have received Christ and are born again. They are made new when they surrender to Christ; born anew, old things having passed away. They are the new container, the new wineskin, carrying Christ Himself within their spirits.

Just as new wine needs a new wineskin, old wine must remain in old wineskins. New and old can't mix; neither can law and grace. The new wine is held in the container of a fresh, new wineskin, just as we hold the truth of Christ Himself. We who are born again symbolize the new wineskin. His blood ratifies the New Testament, giving integrity and truth to grace. Jesus uses this event to contrast the Old Testament law to the New Testament gospel of grace. Old wine can't be transferred to a new container. Nor can a newly made batch of wine be placed in an old container. The Old Testament law was fulfilled in Christ and set aside for a new and everlasting covenant.

Some interpret fasting as a religious act of denial to earn special grace from God. This borders on manipulation and favoritism. Therefore, it becomes a law of works, which has no place in the New Testament. It's not in works of the flesh but rather in works of the heart that God is pleased. It's our faith, obedience, and Christ's righteousness that brings us closer to God. It's turning off the flesh's desire for more of self, withdrawing away from the noise of this world, and spending time alone in God's presence.

Jesus drew away to isolated places, void of distractions, to spend time with the Father. We too must draw away from the demands of anything that replaces quality time in the presence of God. Am I against fasting? No! We are to crucify the dictates of this flesh, so, in essence, fasting should be continual, not an occasional act.

The Weakness of Fasting

New Testament believers can't go back to performing religious works to make themselves righteous. When we do this, we become legalistic. We are saying in essence that what Jesus did wasn't enough, and we have to help the process. It becomes what I can do, not what Jesus did, to be all-sufficient. This is wrong doctrine. It is Christ and Christ alone who has done the perfect work. He has established us in Him to be righteous by faith and not by works. Again, it puts new wine into old wineskins. It mixes the law with grace. Israel fasted, mourned, put on sackcloth, and made animal sacrifices all to show true repentance for their sins. We, as new covenant believers, show true repentance by our faith in Christ, by asking for forgiveness, turning from sin, and being cleansed by Him from all unrighteousness. No amount of fasting can do that.

Fasting doesn't make us more pleasing to God. It's our faith that pleases God. Fasting doesn't make us holy or righteous, nor does it put us in God's good grace. Jesus, who was sinless, took all our sin upon Himself. He became sin. At Calvary, He took our punishment and gave us His righteousness. Our righteousness isn't in fasting or legalistic works. It's in our faith in Christ and His shed blood. It's knowing we have no other way for our sins to be forgiven. We have no hope of eternal life apart from our faith and trust in Jesus.

Fasting doesn't make God answer our prayers. He loves us and hears our prayers. He not only hears our prayers, but He also answers them. They may not be answered in the way we think or desire, but God is always attending to our needs and making provision. Fasting doesn't give us a spiritual breakthrough. Our breakthroughs and answers come by reading God's Word, believing it, and planting the seed of His Word in our hearts by faith.

The Word of God is alive and powerful. Believing the Word and putting our faith and trust in His Word causes us to have a breakthrough. I do not deny the benefits of abstinence. I'm just saying that starving won't make us more holy or closer to God. The truth is we can do nothing to make ourselves more righteous because our righteousness comes from the great exchange at Calvary. Jesus has done it all. We can't add anything to it.

Fasting in the New Covenant of Grace

There is one example of fasting in the new covenant. In the book of Acts, the church at Antioch was worshipping the Lord and fasting. From this the Holy Spirit spoke to them, instructing them to choose both Paul and Barnabus to be sent out as missionaries, establishing churches and preaching the Gospel. As new covenant believers, I believe in seeking the Lord in every decision we make. We need God's wisdom, and we need to hear His voice.

Fasting shuts out the desires of the flesh and allows us to focus on the will of God. Fasting is also believed to be beneficial for our bodies. Rest, sleep, and fasting are ways that the body repairs itself, renews its strength, and regenerates healthy cells. I find I have better sleep when I fast after my evening meal until I awake the next morning. Personally, I have seen benefits to fasting. Before fasting, I would advise consulting with your physician. Fasting food is one way to fast.

If food, hobbies, electronic equipment, or other selfish pursuits take us away from our focus on God, then yes, we should fast those things too, to have time alone with God. Anything that's of the flesh should be brought under the control of the Holy Spirit. Our flesh isn't to dictate to us. Whatever tries to set itself up as an idol for the flesh to worship should not only be avoided but should also be torn down to give God first place in our life. Paul admonishes us to throw off the weights of those sins that so easily beset us.

In conclusion, fasting has its place, but we should remember we are under grace. Jesus said if we loved Him, we would keep His commandments. Being obedient is far better than making sacrifices.

What Is Prayer?

Prayer is communicating with God. It can be formal or informal. Thoughts and words are part of this communication. It can be journaling, studying God's Word, or listening to a sermon. It can even be crying out in frustration at injustice, a sigh, or a deep longing. Look at how a child communicates with their parents. The forms are varied, but it is all communication. Praying effectual prayers comes from the power and wisdom of the Holy Spirit. It can be conversational or formal, sitting or kneeling, long or short. The most important thing is that it's faith filled.

Without the leading and guidance of the Holy Spirit, our prayer life is unfulfilling and one-sided. Prayer is more than presenting our list of needs and wants to God. It's seeking the Kingdom of God first and knowing all these other things will be added to us. If our prayer list is all about ourselves, we have missed the essence of Kingdom life and eternal rewards. The Kingdom of God is more than food and drink and what we wear. It's more than getting the latest electronic device, a better car, a bigger house, expensive clothes, and other material possessions. It is about fulfilling the Great Commission Jesus gave us.

Our goal in prayer is to lay down our will and be conformed to the will of God. Prayer doesn't change God or others; it changes us. Prayer is more than a petition. It's thanksgiving, it's worship, and it's coming into the presence of Almighty God, Creator, and Savior. It's peace and assurance of His great love and care for us. It's the place where we exchange the cares and burdens of this world for the care and provision of the Kingdom of God. It's a place of trust and rest. It's the place where we find direction and answers to our questions. When preparing to minister to others, it's essential we have time alone with God in order to pray for the opportunities that will come. The Bible tells us to be ready in season and out. Fasting is certainly part of the preparation.

As we wake up each day, we have no idea what will come our way. There may be a chance to witness or to pray with someone for healing. The time to pray isn't the moment the need presents itself. We pray, and then go about our day listening to the Holy Spirit for guidance. This prepares us. God will provide opportunities to minister to people, whether at work, or school, or the grocery store, or on the phone. The places and possibilities are endless.

It's vital to our life in the Spirit to have a daily time in His Word and in His presence. This renews our minds to the mind of Christ, sets the focus for the day, and makes us ready to help others. This is what Jesus meant when He said we must eat His flesh and drink His blood. Jesus drew away to be alone on several occasions. He spent time in prayer and in the presence of His Father. If He needed to, how much more do we need to?

Yesterday's anointing won't work for today's need. We need daily bread, fresh revelation. Yesterday's triumph doesn't guarantee today's victory.

Questions

1. What was the reason for fasting in the old covenant? _____ _____ _____

2. What happened if someone did not fast and repent?_____ _____ _____

3. In John 6:48, who does Jesus say He is? _____ _____

4. What does Jesus say we are to feast on as New Testament believers?_____ _____ _____

5. Why did Jesus speak about wineskins in this passage of Scripture?_____ _____ _____

6. Name five things that fasting does not do._____ _____ _____ _____ _____

7. What things could you fast as a new covenant believer that hinders your time with God?_____ _____ _____ _____

8. Do we have to fast food?_____

9. What is prayer?_____ _____

10. What should the goal of prayer be? _____ _____ _____

Reflections: _____

_____

_____

_____

_____

_____

_____

_____

_____

_____

_____

_____

_____

Prayers: _____

_____

_____

_____

_____

_____

_____

_____

_____

_____

_____

_____

_____

Additional Scripture References for Study

Matthew 9:9-17, Hosea 6:6, John 6:27-62, Romans 8:13,
1 Corinthians 11:23-25

Healing the Sick – Releasing the Power of God

Chapter 8 opens with a powerful prophetic message from the Holy Spirit instructing us how to heal the sick. Using it has given me greater results in seeing healings and miracles manifest. It comes near the end of this book because unless we understand the first seven chapters and apply the principles, we won't walk in the victory of healing the sick. God doesn't operate by a formula or rote words. I share how I pray, but believers should build up their own faith by hearing the Holy Spirit speak to them. Healing is not sometime in the future. The Kingdom of God is here within us. God wants to release His love through us to meet the needs of others. Jesus healed us all when He suffered the scourging before the crucifixion. He was bloodied and bruised for our sins. He was chastised for our peace with God. Healing has already been provided for every person through the atonement. It's already waiting to be accessed. We must believe we can access from the realm of the spirit into the realm of the physical.

CHAPTER 8

Healing the Sick – Releasing the Power of God

This prophecy regarding the power of God was given to me in 2017:

Press into Me; push through the distractions of your day. Give Me the first fruits of your day. Seek Me early in the quiet of the morning. I have called each one of you to this place in this hour. There is coming a greater move of My Spirit in the earth than any other time in the history of man. You must know your place in the Body of Christ so that you are rightly fitted together for My purpose. Press into Me with purpose, for as yet you have not made a demand upon My power because you have not understood its meaning nor its potential.

You make requests of Me, but you have not made demands upon My attributes. You have Kingdom rights and tasks to accomplish for preaching and prayer. Press into My presence and make a demand. Even now this saying "make a demand" is foreign to you because you only know of this from a worldly view. But I want you to experience what it means to make a demand upon My power.

When you think of demand, you think of selfishness, of getting your own way, of putting your foot down and pushing your agenda. That is the way of the world. In My Kingdom making a demand becomes how you access My power in helping others, in preaching the Gospel, in being My witness, in healing the sick, and in everything you set out to do with Me. Make a demand when you need anything. Power requires a demand. You make a demand on the electric company's energy when you turn on a switch. Your very action is making a demand. So it is when you seek to heal, to preach, to teach, to deliver. Make a demand for My power and see what greater results you will have.

I told My disciples then as I tell My disciples now, you will receive power when the Holy Spirit has come upon you. I want you to continue to make a demand, on My power. Everything you need has already been supplied. It waits for you in My Kingdom, but you must make a demand on it to bring it from the Kingdom realm to the physical earthly realm. WHATEVER your need, make a demand of My power. Do not demand the thing you need; demand the power. For instance, I give you power to obtain wealth. I don't give you wealth; I give you power to access wealth. This does not mean mere money. That is included as I meet your needs. But it includes life, peace, joy, health, all that you need. So WHATEVER you need or desire for another to meet their needs, make a demand on My power. Make a demand for My power. The miracle is there waiting to be accessed.

My power mixed with your faith is the bridge from the Spirit to the flesh. You do not have to stop and pray and ask Me every time you meet someone else's need. You are not the one meeting the need. The provision for what they need was met at Calvary. ALL that is Mine is yours to freely give to others. I am willing to transfer this provision to others through you AND it comes through My power. You do not have the power to produce results from My Kingdom. What you have residing within you is the very power that raised Christ from the dead. Remember I said, "Apart from Me you can do nothing?" You must make a demand upon My power. Your faith to believe is the switch.

If you can believe, then ALL things are possible to you. You and I are in a partnership. We operate together as one. I am the head and you are the body. You make the demand for what you need; then STAND. You made the demand and I released the power. If there is any hindrance to full recovery, speak to the hindrance and command it to go and never return. You do not need special permission to pray for someone. Jesus did not draw away from the people to be alone and ask Me what things He should do. He knew His assignment by revelation. He came to Me for strength and power. He was one with Me as I and He are one with you.

The Secret Is Faith

In 2009 my thoughts about healing radically changed. I had prayed for the sick for more than twenty years. I approached healing as something God needed to provide instead of realizing He had already provided it. It was already there in the realm of the spirit. Since we were healed two thousand years ago at Calvary, I didn't need to ask God to heal. Healing was already available. Even so, something was missing. How could I get what had been done to do what I needed to be done? I knew there must be a key component. As I sought the Lord, the Holy Spirit began teaching me how to move what was already provided in the Kingdom realm to the realm of the flesh where it was needed.

The prophecy I shared transformed how I prayed, and the results were amazing. In this prophecy, the Holy Spirit says we have a Kingdom right as Christians to make a demand on His power and to ask with authority. We can't heal the sick in our own power, but we can request His power, put our faith in His power, and heal the sick. When we make a demand, we make an insistent and purposeful request. A demand, by the very nature of the word, means something we already have a right to possess. It's not a pious request; it's authoritative, bold, and rightfully ours.

We have the authority, righteousness, and boldness needed to heal the sick. We have the right to be insistent and request something that's rightfully ours. This single sentence, if believed, will give you far greater results as you pray for the sick. The key to laying hold of God's miraculous power is simply to believe in the finished work of Jesus. He fulfilled the law and took upon Himself the curse of sickness and disease. He shed His blood, died, and rose again. He is the Resurrection and the Life. He is seated at the right hand of God with all power and all authority. He has given us His name, His permission, and His will for us to heal the sick.

All sicknesses and diseases are an active form of death. The body part or parts in need of healing are not functioning as they were intended. The life of the organ or system has been invaded with a form of death. As you pray, release your faith in the *power* of God and in His resurrection *life* to flow into the diseased area. Jesus swallowed up death when He rose from the grave. Death no longer has victory because the One who conquered death reigns. He has already provided His life a ransom for all who believe.

There's no formula for healing the sick. There are His power, His life, and our faith coupled with obedience to do what the Holy Spirit instructs. There's no specific prayer or ten-step program. There are His commands and our obedience. The secret we are all looking for is simply *faith;* faith in His Word and in His power. The purpose of this book is to teach and grow your confidence so you can heal the sick. If there were a specific prayer or formula, I wouldn't have written all nine chapters of this book. The chapters were written and designed by the Holy Spirit to bring you on the path to truth and strengthen your faith.

You might think, *Is it all my faith, or is it all the person's faith, or is it some of both?* The answer is YES! The New Testament tells story after story of people coming to Jesus to be healed. They came to the synagogue, to the market, to the roadside, to the houses where He dined, to the mountainside where He preached, and to the shores of the Sea of Galilee. They asked to touch His garment; they asked Him to come to their house and raise the dead; they asked Him to send the Word to their servant; to cast the demon out of their child; to open their blind eyes; to heal their paralysis; and to make their leprous skin clean. Jesus lived among many people with many needs. Certainly, their faith in Him played a part in receiving from Him. Jesus, in His own hometown, did not do many mighty miracles because of their *unbelief*. But did those without faith receive from Jesus? What about those with unbelief?

For example, what about the faith of the friends who removed the roof from the housetop and lowered the man down on a bed? What about Jairus's daughter who was dead, or the widow of Nain whose son was dead, or Lazarus? Was it their faith or His faith? What about the Gadarene demoniac or the man's son whom the disciples couldn't heal? Was it their faith or Jesus's faith? And what about the man who said, "I believe, help my unbelief"? Faith and compassion are keys, whether it's their faith or your faith. Faith and compassion are required.

If faith is required, how much faith should we have? How many people should we get on the prayer chain? How many churches and ministries need to pray? We have this notion the more people we get praying, the more God will answer our request. God is not deaf, He doesn't need a crowd, but He demands faith. Prayer isn't about how much and how many. Jesus said a tiny speck of faith could move a mountain. He also said we only need to find one other person to agree with us and we could have what we asked.

I think the problem is we confuse the "mountains." Our thoughts grasp the mountain concept, but then we get our eyes focused on the mountain of the problem. We tend to think a mountain-sized amount of faith is needed to move a mountain-sized problem. So we set out to gather a lot of people. The bigger the problem and the more desperate the need, panic sets in and we forget what Jesus said. We look at the mountain of a problem and start calling friends and prayer groups, prayer lines, and call centers. Now, instead of moving the mountain with a small amount of faith and one other person, we create another mountain. We think the bigger the mountain of people praying the better.

Can you see this is really unbelief and does not line up with what Jesus taught? Faith only needs to be less than an inch in size, and we only need one other believer to agree with us. Jesus said if we have these two things, we can ask and receive what we desire. It's so simple we miss it. These two things, a small amount of faith and one other believer, will move the mountain. When Jesus sent out the disciples and told them to heal the sick, He sent them out two by two. He did not send out the entire group as one big unit! The Word says if two people agree, it shall be done. We don't need to get a mountain to move a mountain. So, if the amount of faith needed is small and the number of people praying is two, why don't we see the sick healed and the dead raised? I believe the answer is unbelief.

What Is the Difference between Doubt and Unbelief?

Doubt is not unbelief. Doubt only becomes unbelief when given full attention and submission. Doubt is either a stepping-stone to unbelief or a springboard to faith. The decision is ours through the gift of free will. Every person has times of doubt. Doubt is the normal result of thinking and processing, being too analytical, and looking inward instead of looking upward. Doubt has to be fed to grow. If doubt is allowed to grow it will be eventually bear the fruit of unbelief. Doubt is intrinsic to every human being. How we deal with doubt either causes us to push beyond and reach for faith or go in the opposite direction, which leads to unbelief.

Both doubt and unbelief negate faith. Doubt is rooted in distrust of someone or something. One of the great tragedies of the fall of Adam and Eve occurred when they ate the fruit of the Tree of the Knowledge of Good and Evil. They instantly knew right from wrong and obedience from disobedience. Their sin brought guilt, shame, blame, and separation. The enemy planted seeds of doubt, which he quickly manipulated into unbelief and then to disobedience. Trust was broken between man and God, paving the way for the darkness of doubt and unbelief.

As human beings, we learn early to live by our five senses. We believe what we can see, hear, smell, touch, and taste. They are our sensory perception of the world around us. As believers, we are admonished to be led by the Holy Spirit. This life of faith and trust in the Holy Spirit can develop into a sense stronger than our five human senses. I attribute this growth to the truth of the Word of God, meditating on His Word, believing, and obeying. When doubt comes, I find it best to get rid of it before it gets a foothold. I do this through the promises of God and putting my trust in Him. When we've been made perfect in the love of God, we won't doubt. We will trust the One who loves us completely and perfectly.

Faith and Trust versus Doubt and Unbelief

In healing the sick, you will come up against doubt in two ways. One is the person's doubt, and the other is your doubt. *First*, we'll look at the doubt of the person who needs healing. Let's say you are ministering to a person with a diagnosis of cancer. They desperately want to be healed and have spent hours researching a cure, looking at statistics for longevity, and believing what their senses perceive. They will listen to death speaking through the physician's words, the imaging reports, blood work numbers, and even well-meaning friends and family. The longer this behavior is fed, the stronger it grows, which is why I believe we don't see more miracles of healing.

The computer is the information highway. We can't spend hours piling up unbelief and then expect a miracle. It won't work. The unbelief chokes out the Word of God and makes it of no effect. The miracle doesn't originate in the flesh. It originates in the spirit and manifests in the flesh. If the flesh is stronger than the spirit, unbelief will be stronger than faith. If a person spends time reading and meditating on healing Scriptures, their doubt won't grow. Instead, their faith will arise. They will believe God's Word above what the doctor's report says, and healing will occur. I'm not saying deny a sickness. I'm saying deny sickness the atmosphere to grow. I'm saying what we hear and what we read governs the outcome of the situation.

Why is it important to *speak* the Word of God? Faith comes by hearing and hearing by the Word of God. The Word strengthens our spirit, and a strong spirit overcomes the flesh. Speaking the Word enacts the covenant ratified in the blood of Jesus. When we speak, we make an agreement in the earth with the Word of God. In other words, we declare the Word to be truth over what our senses perceive. The Word of God is alive and resides in our spirits. We must learn how to reach into our spirit and access faith in the Word of God. We can't do this if we are feeding our senses. The Word of God is seed, and the miracle we need is within that seed. We have God's Word, His authority, and His power working through us. Our part is to believe and speak forth our miracle.

The *second* type of doubt is our own doubt. We can get our eyes on the illness and its manifestations much like Peter did while walking on water. He started out well but fell because he allowed what he saw and heard to cause doubt. When a person comes for healing, you will be tempted to look at the sickness and hear their words of doubt and unbelief. You must look beyond what you see in the natural and insistently make a demand on the power of God to heal their illness. Remember, the worst case of cancer is as easy for Jesus to heal as the slightest little malady.

Nothing is impossible for God if we can only believe. Our faith determines the outcome. We can't let what we see with our eyes, hear with our ears, and feel with our touch to be greater than our faith in the power of God to heal. I believe those are two critical keys in healing the sick. It's Jesus's power, His life, and His will coupled with our faith in Him. There's not one event in the Bible in which Jesus lacked either the power or the desire to heal a person. The only lack came from their unbelief.

Healing Is Now

When we heal the sick, we must remember that healing isn't in the future. In other words, we aren't waiting in the sweet by-and-by for healing *someday*. God's power and His desire are available constantly twenty-four seven. God's not healing anyone today. He healed two thousand years ago when He hung on the cross. It was part of the whole package of the atonement. So, if God isn't healing anyone today, how do we get healed? It's a matter of faith and the knowledge that the Kingdom of God is within us. Faith in God and what

He's done is the key to receive what's already ours. The Bible says we were healed, not we are going to be healed.

It's not healing we need; it's the manifestation of the atonement. That manifestation is exerted and made visible through the nine gifts of the Holy Spirit. The Holy Spirit brings what has already been provided from the supernatural realm to the natural realm. It becomes a matter of demonstration and manifestation because the Kingdom of God is not up there somewhere. It's right here, within every believer.

When we heal the sick, it's through the power of the Kingdom of God that resides within us. The very power that raised Christ from the dead dwells in us. If the power of God could raise Christ from the dead, then that's all the power we need to heal the sick. The Kingdom of God isn't an external place. The King of glory has taken up residence in our spirits. All we need for life and godliness are supplied by His *resident presence*. Resident presence refers to the Kingdom of God that resides within each believer.

When the Holy Spirit gave me the words *resident presence*, I had a picture of Queen Elizabeth's royal standard flag which is flown above whatever residence she currently occupies. Her personal flag with its emblems and colors is time-honored and displays her sovereignty and authority. It's a sign to everyone Her Majesty resides within. Our King Jesus, who is King of Kings and Lord of Lords, resides and makes His home within all of us who make Him our Lord. Not only is King Jesus in residence, but He too has a royal standard, which flies above us. We are known in the Kingdom of God. We are protected and comforted. We are His and His banner over us is love.

What If I Pray and Nothing Happens?

If you don't pray, nothing will happen. But what if you pray and the person is fully healed? Keep praying. It's those who knock and keep on knocking, ask, and keep on asking, seek, and keep on seeking, that receive. God rewards those who diligently seek Him. If you're serious about your desire to see the sick healed, heal them in the name of Jesus and in the power of the Kingdom of God. Let God see that you earnestly want to heal the sick. Would you risk praying five times with no results to see a miracle the sixth time you pray? When God sees your diligent seeking of Him, He will reward you.

I have prayed for people in the hospital, at work, at home, in the church, at the store, at the beauty shop, and at the gas station. I have prayed on the phone, in a text, in an email, and in a letter. Keep praying for the sick! Our responsibility is to have faith in God and faith in His power residing in us. It's not our kingdom, although we live in it. It's not our power, although we operate in it. We are the vessel God flows through. The secret, which is no secret, is to *believe*. Have faith and compassion. Jesus instructed His disciples to go out and freely give what He had given them. We are His disciples and are to freely give the gift of faith and healing to those in need. Freely you've received; freely give.

My Job, God's Responsibility

A vessel is just that, a container that holds something. We are less than useful vessels because we leak and have to be continually refilled. Who would reach for a pitcher that leaks? A pitcher like that isn't useful to us, but God views things differently. I believe our cracks and leakiness are by design. They keep us dependent on the One who uses us. They remind us we have no power in and of ourselves. They remind us of who's in control. Can we clean ourselves, fill ourselves, and pour ourselves out? No, we are fit only to be useful in the Master's hand. It humbles us when we know that even though we are cracked, we are useful to God. Even though we aren't a fine-cut glass crystal vase, but an earthen jar, the Kingdom of God has chosen to reside in us.

Practical Examples of How to Heal the Sick

When I pray for someone, I lay my hands on them. Jesus told us to do that in Mark 16:17-18. Many times, people will tell me my hands are hot and the warmth feels good. That's the Holy Spirit, not me. Jesus said, we shall lay hands on…then He said, they shall recover… *We shall, so they shall!* If the area of sickness is in a private part of the body, I lay my hands on their shoulders or hold their hands. If I can touch their body part, I put one hand on the front and one on the back of the part. This isn't a rule; it's just what I do. The Holy Spirit will show me where the pain is and if it's natural or demonic. If the pain is physical, I speak to the body part and strengthen it with love and care. I say:

> *Body part (name the part, like knee or arm), I have good news for you. Jesus has already healed you and now your healing is going to manifest. I come to strengthen you and thank you for working as well as you can. The Bible says, in the name of Jesus, I shall lay hands on the sick, and they shall recover. I am going to lay my hands on you now. Holy Spirit, I make a demand on Your power and I set my faith to Your power right now. The Kingdom of God is here. Jesus, I release Your power and Your life into this area (name the body part or the disease). I take authority over this sickness and command it to leave your body, in the name of Jesus. I forbid you, sickness, to return to this person. Jesus, I release my faith and Your resurrection life to flow through me to this area in need and bring health and total restoration to it. Sickness, you have no authority here. Jesus and I have all authority and power over you. Leave now. Devil, you release the stronghold you have over this person right now, in Jesus's name. I curse the plan you have to kill, steal, and destroy. You shall not execute your plan over this body anymore. These are the signs that follow those that believe: in My name, they shall lay hands on the sick and the sick shall recover.*

I command the life and wholeness of Jesus to go from the top of your head to the soles of your feet. Be made whole right now, in the name of Jesus. Amen.

Next, I ask people to do something they couldn't do previously. I ask about their pain and how they feel. Sometimes the Holy Spirit manifests in feelings of warmth, energy, joy, or laughter. I ask them if Jesus is their Lord and Savior. If He's not, I lead them in the prayer at the front of this book. If they acknowledge Jesus is Lord, I ask them if they've received the baptism of the Holy Spirit and if they would like to and I lead them in prayer. I also take a few minutes to tell them the importance of holding on to their healing. I say this:

The devil may come back and try to convince you that you are not healed. He will give you thoughts and say that all this is foolishness and nothing happened. He may even give you a pain, and it may be stronger than ever before. This is his deceitfulness. He is a liar. Don't believe him. You were healed. The devil wants you to come into agreement with his deception. He wants you to give away your faith in God and the healing that the Holy Spirit manifested in you. If the pain returns, you must speak to it and confess your healing and command the devil and the sickness to leave. Then begin to praise God and thank Him for healing you. Say, "Thank You, Jesus. I know You healed me and the devil is a liar." Tell Him you believe He healed you. The devil will leave you alone once you start praising God because the Bible says that God inhabits the praises of His people.

Pain may not be specific or physical. Sometimes it is emotional or vague. People don't always know why they feel bad. They may even say that the doctors can't find the problem. If there's no known disease but pain and debilitation, I take authority over an unclean spirit. Jesus rebuked unclean spirits and told His disciples to cast out devils in His name. I say:

Holy Spirit, I make a demand on Your power and Your authority over the devil. I come against you, unclean spirit, and forbid you to stay in this person. I rebuke depression, fear, anxiety, and nervousness. I command you to come out in the name of Jesus and never return. I forbid you to return to this person. I curse your plan to steal, kill, and destroy. You will not execute your plan any longer. I command you to go, in Jesus's name. Holy Spirit, I ask You to manifest with peace and truth and life in Jesus. In Jesus's name. Amen.

As with physical healings and miracles, I ask people how they feel. Many times, they say that whatever was there is now gone. I also caution them, as I previously stated, what to do if the enemy tries to return.

These are just examples of how I pray. The most important thing is to listen carefully to the Holy Spirit and do what He tells you to do. He will give you what is needed for the person. I also ask about salvation and the baptism of the Holy Spirit. The key is to listen to the directions and promptings of the Holy Spirit and act on what He is telling you. Faith must have works. My work is to do what the Holy Spirit says. Their work is to respond. That's why I ask them to do something they could not previously do after the healing has manifested.

If you are using this text as a teaching manual for study groups, I would like to encourage you to "role play" with each other. You can break into teams and pray for one another. I have seen this done and people in the group are healed. If you would like more help with this exercise, please contact me at Milliemcilvaine@yahoo.com and I will be happy to help your group.

Healing for Yourself

Perhaps you bought this book because you are sick. Maybe you have a terminal illness and want to be healed. The good news of the Gospel is that Jesus has already healed you. The same power to heal others is the same power to heal yourself. All that is required is faith. Using the examples in this chapter, this is how I pray for myself when I am sick. I lay my hands on the body part that needs healing and say the following words:

> *Father, I thank You for providing healing for me. Holy Spirit, I ask You to manifest the gift of miracles and healings in me right now. I believe You want me well. I believe You love me and have a good plan for my life. Your Word says that if I lay hands on the sick and ask in Your name, Jesus, I will recover. So now by faith, I lay my hands on my body. I make a demand on Your power and put my faith in Your power and Your resurrection life. These are the signs that follow those that believe: in My name, they shall lay hands on the sick, and they shall recover. I am laying my hands on myself, and I believe I will live and recover from this disease and illness. Holy Spirit, please manifest now so that I can be well. Jesus, I thank You for healing me. I know that You were beaten and crucified, and because of Your death and resurrection I am healed. I believe You. I believe I am healed. Thank You, Holy Spirit, for healing me right now. In Jesus's name. Amen.*

Continue to confess your healing. Begin to move and do something you could not previously do. Resist the devil's lie that you are sick and dying. Take, by faith, what is yours in Christ Jesus. If you have never received Jesus as your Lord and Savior, now is the time to do so. There is a prayer in the front of the book. Pray it with a sincere desire and God will make you born again and give you eternal life.

Questions

1. What does the Holy Spirit tell us we can make a demand upon? _____
   _____
   _____

2. Why is it our right as believers to make a demand on the power of God? _____
   _____
   _____

3. How big does our faith need to be in order to heal the sick? _____
   _____

4. How many people need to come into agreement with our prayer of faith? _____

5. Is doubt the same as unbelief, why? _____
   _____
   _____
   _____

6. Where is the Kingdom of God located? _____

7. Can our five senses negate our faith for healing? How? _____
   _____
   _____
   _____

8. If I command sickness to leave and it does not, should I quit commanding? _____

9. In the Great Commission, we are told to perform miracles. By whose authority and
   name do we do this? _____

10. What is the secret to healing the sick?_____

Reflections: _____

_____

_____

_____

_____

_____

_____

_____

_____

_____

_____

_____

_____

Prayers: _____

_____

_____

_____

_____

_____

_____

_____

_____

_____

_____

_____

_____

_____

Additional Scripture References for Study

Luke 17:20-21, John 14:16-17, 1 John 4:4, Ephesians 3:20-21,
Philippians 2:13, Psalm 60:4-5, Song of Solomon 2:4, Isaiah 49:22,
Matthew 10:8, Matthew 18:19

Walking in and Speaking Health

Chapter 9 begins with another prophetic word from the Holy Spirit. Our life in Christ is often described as a walk of faith. God has ordained faith to be vital in receiving from Him. All that God created He created by speaking it into existence. Words have power. They can bring death or life. There are no words more powerful than speaking Scripture over circumstances. Jesus rebuked Satan by quoting Scripture. God's Word is powerful because it's Spirit and life. When we speak over a person, we enact God's promise to heal by putting our faith in His power and in His Word.

CHAPTER 9

Walking in and Speaking Health

This prophecy regarding redemption and healing was given to me in 2017:

Many times in the life of My servants, I allow doors to close, plans to fail, and dreams to shatter. I risk being misunderstood and even forsaken and accused. If My people would only fully trust Me and completely surrender, they would see it is not an end but rather a glorious beginning. Pain and suffering are stepping-stones to joy and freedom. When I created color, I made variety. When I created flowers, I made variety. When I created mankind, I created variety. I did not make one color, one flower, or one man. Purple is as necessary as red, blue, or green. Music is more than one note and songs are more than one word. All things I created are varied in size, color, and purpose, and yet man desires the same one-dimensional choice. That choice is always pleasure without pain, abundance without lack, and joy without sorrow. No one seeks Me for sorrow; no one asks for lack.

The struggle in life is for man to live a life devoid of anything unpleasant. He cannot see beyond what his senses feel, and he lacks the wisdom to traverse the valley to reach the mountaintop. If man would trust Me and think good of Me when suffering and sorrow come; if he would rejoice at the barren condition of his soul and trust Me, he would see My plan of redemption, healing, and deliverance. The journey would be less difficult, and the weight would be light, yet man does not believe I and I alone know the way. I AM the Way. I have prepared pleasures for each person, but they must come on the way with Me to obtain them.

Every blessing, every joy, every good thing is My agenda for your life, yet you do not believe Me when trouble comes. Don't you know trouble is inevitable? Don't you understand I and I alone have overcome all these things? Trouble is merely a stepping-stone to cross, not a valley where you encamp. You make the journey difficult because in your desire to escape trouble, you desert Me and in doing so you prolong the days of your agony. I embraced My cross because it was the way to glory. Whatever trial you face today, you can make it a stepping-stone to glory or a campground of misery and defeat.

If you hear My voice today, do not harden your heart in unbelief and indifference. I AM the Way, the Truth, and the Life. Believe Me when I tell you, no matter what circumstance you find yourself in, nothing is too difficult, no path too hard, for My steps. I have already gone ahead of you and laid up every provision for your life. The key to unlock this treasure is trust and obedience.

Death and Life

Proverbs 18:21 (KJV)
Death and life are in the power of the tongue: and they that love it shall eat the fruit thereof.

Our words matter, and they have significant bearing on our future. They are the creative force for life and blessing or death and cursing. Little phrases like, "This drives me crazy," or "I am scared to death," or "I am so poor I can't even pay attention," may seem innocent or even humorous at times, but they have far more power than we think. They sound simple, but they're shaping our future. When we speak, we're either entering a covenant with life or with death. Many healings have been lost because of what was spoken following the manifestation.

When Jim and I were first married, we lived paycheck to paycheck. I wrote out our offering check and paid the bills. There was always just enough to cover the expenses. One day, we decided to "speak to that checkbook." I held it up in the air, thanked God for what we had, and said, "We are rich beyond what this checkbook says." Every time we received a paycheck, we said the same thing. We didn't just say words; we believed the words we spoke. Not long after that, we had enough money to put a down payment on our first house. We not only spoke out prosperity to build a home, but we also spoke out the household items we needed. A year later we moved in. It was beautifully decorated, like pages from a magazine. I know it came from speaking faith-filled words and believing what we said would come to pass.

We don't appreciate the power of our words. They activate the spirit world and bring life or death into our situations. It's easy to be careless with words, especially if we don't think they have power. It was the spoken Word that created the heavens and the earth. Jim and I have spoken the Word over our finances, our future, our health, and our ministry work.

We have seen God move our nothing into His something. All things have been provided for us. I believe God has stored up provision for all of us that we never use because we don't believe it exists. There is a world beyond our five senses, a place where our needs are met. Speaking brings what has already been provided in the spirit to meet what we need in the natural, if we'll speak life and believe.

The Bible teaches a lot about faith. It comes by hearing the Word of God and by speaking the Word to our situation. Our tongue is a powerhouse for good or for evil. It creates life or death, provision or lack. It's not merely speaking positive things. It's speaking God's Word and believing what we say will come to pass. It's aligning our words and thoughts with what God says. If He says we were healed, then it's truth.

If we put our faith in truth and speak out His Words, we'll have what we need, including our healing. Speaking is only part of the process. We must also believe what we say. When God created the heavens and the earth, He spoke all things into existence. He didn't say, "Let there be" and hoped it would happen. No, He said, "Let there be" and it happened. So it is with us. Empty declarations are fruitless *unless faith is applied*. Rote sayings have no power to produce miracles, but our faith in His Word has power.

The Word Is at Work

We aren't waiting for God to heal us. When I understood this, it changed how I prayed for the sick. God is waiting for us to receive what He did two thousand years ago on Calvary's cross. I am not asking God to heal; I am receiving healing. There is a huge difference in asking for something and receiving something. His goodness and grace have provided all we need or will ever need. When we speak in line with God's finished work on the cross, power goes forth. God's Words are not empty, meaningless, impotent containers. God is a spirit, and it's the Spirit who gives life.

Every time Jesus spoke, He spoke *life* where death had previously reigned. He spoke, and the death of blindness gave forth to life and vision. The death of paralysis gave forth to life and movement. The death of an inadequate amount of a few fish and loaves gave forth to life and nourishment. A dead corpse gave forth to resurrected life and glory. The Word always works because it is Spirit and Life.

God's Word is active and full of life. His Word is forever sealed in heaven. When God speaks, His Word goes forth and doesn't return without producing what pleases Him and what accomplishes His purpose and will. His Word prospers in the situation to which He sends it. If God's Word is all-powerful, we should put our faith into it, speak it, and expect to see results. It's not the voice that works; it's the Word that works. When we pray Scripture over a sick person, we're doing what Jesus did. We're speaking life to places where death previously reigned.

When we grasp the glory of His Word, speak it out, and believe it, great miracles come forth. We have His promise and guarantee. Our existence is by the spoken Word of God. Our covenant position in the earth is to establish God's Kingdom. The Word of God is alive and sharper than a two-edged sword. It cuts death away and brings life. It moves provision from the spirit realm to the physical realm. Jesus quoted Scripture when He taught in the temple, when He privately taught His disciples, when He spoke in parables to the multitudes, and when He was tempted by the devil. He spoke life where death tried to reign. If the Word worked for Jesus, it will work for us as we minister to the sick in His name.

Lifestyles

Certainly, lifestyles play a role in keeping our healing. God meets us in our need, heals us, and expects us to continue to walk free from the bondage of sickness. The moment we are healed, the door to the enemy is shut. If it reopens, we are the ones who open it.

Repentance is a turning away from sin with a change-of-heart attitude and lifestyle. If we are really sorry for what we did, we won't do it again. We are to show the fruit of repentance. That means people should see a change in us and in our behavior. It is an outward manifestation of our hearts being changed. What once was sinful and pleasurable won't appeal to us. We will walk away from the old lifestyle for a new and better one.

Being healed of a disease caused by our lifestyle isn't a license to continue in that lifestyle. We are free to walk out of the disease, but not free to continue in it unharmed. When Jesus rescued the woman caught in the act of adultery, He told her to go on her way and stop sinning. When Jesus sets us free, we aren't free to return to the former lifestyle that put us in bondage and sickness:

> **Matthew 12:43-45 (KJV)**
> **43 When the unclean spirit is gone out of a man, he walketh through dry places, seeking rest, and findeth none. 44 Then he saith, I will return into my house from whence I came out; and when he is come, he findeth it empty, swept, and garnished. 45 Then goeth he, and taketh with himself seven other spirits more wicked than himself, and they enter in and dwell there: and the last state of that man is worse than the first. Even so shall it be also unto this wicked generation.**

In this passage of Scripture, Jesus speaks of a man delivered from an unclean spirit. He makes a point to say the unclean spirit has a will and ability to possess a man. The unclean spirit returns to the place it had previously occupied and finds three things: the house is unoccupied, swept, and garnished. Verse 44 is of particular note. The house it came from appears to be in order, but on further investigation, the place is unoccupied (empty). Because of the emptiness, the spirit takes seven other spirits more wicked than himself. They all find an entry and dwell there, and the man's condition is worse than in the beginning.

Once we've been set free, the enemy will come back to tempt us again. Our house is no longer his house. We can do all the right things, but if Jesus doesn't occupy our house, the enemy has a means to come back. The Holy Spirit spoke these words to me for you as you heal the sick.

> *My child, as you move into this new ministry of healing, you must be aware of the enemy's trickery and deception. As you train the teams, teach them spiritual warfare. Be prepared for an attack. The same authority you use against the enemy is the same authority you use against sickness and disease. Learning to discern My voice is critical.*

The Enemy's Trickery and Deception

The devil will always try to come back to ground he once held. After tempting Jesus, Satan departed, but he returned at a more opportune time. He is powerless, yet subtle and crafty. The only power he has is the power we give him. We allow him to return by our words. He plants the thoughts of doubt in our mind, gives us a symptom, and then waits for us to speak and agree with him. Our "house" must not only be in order, but it must also be occupied by Jesus.

Don't believe the devil's lies and deception. Submit to God. Resist the devil, and he will go away. The devil is a liar. Jesus called him the father of lies. Eventually he will get tired of being pierced with the sword of the Word of God. When you quote Scripture to the devil you pierce him with God's Word. Eventually he will get the hint, and he will leave you alone. He is testing you to see if you will allow him to come back. You were healed, so stand on that truth. Put your faith in the power of God and believe God wants you well. Sickness is never from God. It's the result of living in a fallen world, giving into temptation, and sinning. It comes from the devil.

Another weapon of the enemy is imagery. You'll recognize this as his attempt to defeat and destroy your faith. He uses powerful, mental images coupled with a spirit of fear. The images are always death and destruction. An abnormal pain or symptom in your body is followed by a drastic self-diagnosis of death or impending doom. If you lose a job or owe bills with no backup savings, the devil's imagery is foreclosure, homelessness, and living under a bridge. If you receive a bad report from the physician, he immediately sends images of suffering and sure death. None of these images are from God. He is the giver of life, not the destroyer. If the devil can get you to feed on destructive thoughts and fear, he gains a foothold in the situation. Once he's been successful with fear, he plants doubt, which if believed, turns to unbelief.

You Are in a Spiritual Battle

Many years ago I was in bondage to fear. After coming to Jesus, I began to pray and ask the Holy Spirit to deliver me from this fear. Here are some of the lessons I learned on spiritual warfare.

The Bible calls fear a spirit, or a spirit of fear, and it clearly states that God does not give us this spirit. He does, however, give us power and love and soundness of mind. The devil brings chaos and fear, feelings of hopelessness, and being out of control. He wants to isolate us and make us believe that God is displeased with us. He attacks our thoughts, causing us to be unsure and unstable in thinking and understanding.

> **2 Timothy 1:7 (NKJV)**
> **For God has not given us a spirit of fear, but of power and of love and of a sound mind.**

You have authority and power over the devil in the name of Jesus. If you experience fear or are fearful, you can speak to that spirit of fear and command it to leave. This Scripture is excellent to stand on, put your faith in, and speak out whenever you feel anxious, overwhelmed, or afraid. Remember, you are in a battle, but God through the power of His Word will make you victorious. Here is an example of how to pray against the spirit of fear:

> *You foul spirit of fear, I command you to leave me right now, in the name of Jesus. God's Word says that He gives me power, love, and a sound mind. Depart from me and do not return. I have power over you in the name of Jesus. I have His love and His mind. Leave right now, in the name of Jesus. Amen.*

Demonic spirits cooperate with one another and move as a group. For example, the spirit of addiction operates with a spirit of lying and deceitfulness. Usually, there is a "con man" spirit of manipulation working as well. Sneaking around, hiding evidence of the addiction, and stealing also accompany this group.

Demonic spirits of fear, doubt, and unbelief also operate in a group. Fear is the first and strongest spirit. It arrives with force, imagery, and a form of paralysis. It knocks on the door the loudest and is the most relentless. If you suffer from fear, know that you have authority in the name of Jesus to cast away this spirit. Once fear has a foothold it makes way for the next spirit, which is doubt. Doubt is weaker than fear but more sinister. Doubt raises questions in our minds as to God's goodness and mercy. Finally, when fear and doubt enter, they usher in unbelief. Unbelief is the weakest of the threesome but by far the deadliest. The devil's aim is to steal your faith by attacking you with unbelief.

Spiritual warfare is the fight of every believer because we have an adversary. That adversary has been defeated by Jesus. We have His name and His promises. We are more than conquerors in Christ Jesus.

What If the Symptoms Return?

The enemy may try to tempt you into believing you weren't healed. He does this through pain or a form of hindrance associated with previous symptoms. Sometimes the attack is forceful. Remember, he has no power or authority other than what you give him. Speak to the pain, symptom, or hindrance and command it to go in Jesus's name. This is how I pray:

> *Devil, I am not taking this sickness back into my body, I am healed by the stripes of Jesus. I speak to this counterattack plan you have to steal, kill, and destroy, and I curse your plan and call it to naught (failed). You will not execute your plan over me, my family, or any of the things God has given me, in the name of Jesus. Jesus came that I might have life and have it in abundance. Depart from me and never return. In Jesus's name. Amen.*

Stay in the Word

God's Word is truth. Every promise made in the Bible is upheld by God Himself. His Word is pure. There is no illusion, deceit, darkness, or misrepresentation in His Word. The world changes, people change, but God's Word is absolute. You can trust God's promises because they are a sure guarantee. God is not trying to set traps, manipulate, or harm us. God is love, and the Bible is His message to the world of that love. God purposes good for our life and invites us to come into His presence. He will lead us if we trust Him and allow Him to take control of our lives. The answer to every need is found in the Bible.

In 2007 my husband was diagnosed with a spiculated mass in his lung and given the diagnosis of lung cancer. I saw his X-rays and read the CAT scan report. I spent forty-five years in the field of radiology and have looked at thousands of chest X-rays. Everything on a chest X-ray that appears black is air and everything that appears white is solid structures. A normal chest X-ray should have all black lungs with white rib shadows demonstrated. A tumor or fluid is white and shouldn't be in the airspace of the lungs. Every time I prayed for Jim, I saw the image of the tumor. One night I read Psalm 91. It was a very familiar passage of Scripture and one that gave me great comfort and peace:

> **Psalm 91:5-6 (AMPC, emphasis added)**
> **You shall not be afraid of the terror of the night, nor of the arrow (the evil plots and slanders of the wicked) that flies by day, ⁶*Nor of the pestilence that stalks in darkness*, nor of the destruction and sudden death that surprise *and* lay waste at noonday.**

As soon as I read verse 6, I immediately connected the X-ray image to the Word. The darkness or (blackness) that should be on the chest X-ray and a pestilence (cancer) had stalked into his chest in the form of a tumor. I identified with the Word of God and received it as truth. I believed the Holy Spirit had shown me specific Scripture for healing. I closed my eyes and prayed for my husband. This time there was no white tumor. All I saw was normal black density on the X-ray. Three months later, he had a follow-up chest X-ray and it was completely normal. There was no tumor.

Seeing Yourself Healed

All miracles are manifestations of the Holy Spirit. As human beings, we lack the creative ability to produce a miracle. Coupled with this lack, our thought process is tied to our experiences. We can't experience the future because we live in a fixed period of time. The future is framed by our past; it serves as a reference point. We dream and desire future plans, but we are unable to leave the present to experience the future.

Part of the healing process is to *visualize* the sickness removed and health restored to the area in need. Faith must look beyond what the natural eye sees. I learned something valuable. Seeing the miracle manifest in the spirit is part of bringing the supernatural to the natural realm. The healing is there in the realm of the spirit, purchased by Christ at His scourging. We must connect with the Word of God and believe it as more truthful than what our eyes see or our senses perceive. The Word of God worked in the specific instance for my husband's healing as I received it and saw it.

Another important aspect of healing is revelation. I believe familiar Scriptures can become rote prayers rather than revelation knowledge. It becomes rote because as we study God's Word and apply it to our lives, it takes on a meaning for a particular situation. We build faith by allowing the Word to move us to victory. However, as I have previously stated, we are tied to our experiences.

Psalm 91 was one of the first Scriptures I learned as a new Christian. I had always loved it because it brought me peace and stability. I never saw it as a healing Scripture, but rather a Scripture of protection. However, on this occasion, it brought the miracle my husband needed. It was the *revelation* of the Word applied to the need that changed the situation from death to life. From now on, this new revelation of Psalm 91 will be a constant reminder of Jim's miracle. I can't read it without tying it to my experience.

The problem's not the Word failing to work; it's my limitation to move beyond the past. We need fresh manna (fresh revelation) from the Word of God. Remember in chapter 7, we are to continually feast on His flesh and blood. Jesus didn't say, "Come and have one meal with Me, but rather *abide* in Me and grow from revelation to revelation."

The Kingdom of God grows within our understanding because of revelation knowledge. God isn't a formula to be figured out. He isn't an equation to solve. He builds His Kingdom within us through the fresh revelation of His Word. We can't live on yesterday's triumph. I have come to know God doesn't meet our needs the same way every time. His mercies are new every day.

Compassion for the Body

Recently the Holy Spirit gave me a new revelation. I used this revelation to bring healing to a person with sixty-two years of chronic, recurrent bowel obstructions. I heard the Holy Spirit tell me to lay hands on a specific area and speak to that portion of the bowel. Always obey His voice, even if it sounds strange, because it's a step of faith. As I laid my hands on the person's abdomen, I was impressed to speak and declare the good news of the Gospel to the area of intense pain. This is especially true if there's a long-standing chronically weakened portion of the body.

In that moment of obedience, I was flooded with intense feelings of love and compassion. It was as though that portion of the colon was trying its best to function properly but was simply too weak, too tired, and too sick. There's a time to be bold and command the sickness to leave, but there's also a place for love mixed with faith. This is a key to success in praying for people or for yourself to be healed of chronic ailments. Here's what I mean.

There is a natural tendency on the part of an injured or sick person to despise not only their sickness but also the affected part of their body. Desiring to be rid of the ongoing ailment, they unknowingly speak death over it. We say things like, "I wish I didn't have this body," or "Why do I have this constant issue?" Both mentally and verbally we express our displeasure with the malfunctioning part and even come to a place of loathing the condition and blaming the inefficiency of the body part to do its job.

God created all parts of our bodies: the ones seen and the ones unseen. He created them to function together and to come to the rescue of one another for health and life. My hand may be beautifully adorned with jewelry, but is it more important than the hidden parts of my digestive tract? Can I say, "Hand, I need you, and you are beautiful to me," yet curse or reject a weaker part of the body and treat it with contempt?

In praying for the person to be healed of the current obstruction, the Holy Spirit showed me the area needing help, strength, and reinforcement. I spoke and declared that Jesus had died and that this part of the body would live long and strong. Immediately, the intense abdominal pain subsided, and within the hour, all function was restored to normal. This was indeed a true miracle because the person had suffered from birth, having reconstructive surgery at a few hours old. All their life they had suffered with bowel surgeries and ongoing issues. Each one of them required hospitalization and medical procedures. This time the Lord supernaturally healed the bowel and restored all function without any human intervention. The Holy Spirit manifested His gift in the working of a miracle.

I believe our bodies, created by God in His image and likeness, work in harmony and desire to function and serve us as God wills. I also believe they become weak and need strengthening. If our words are death and disgust, the problem becomes chronic, not due to the body part being rebellious, but rather due to our speaking death over it.

In Conclusion

I urge you to stay in God's Word, listen to the Holy Spirit, and do what He tells you to do. The Word works. I could tell you testimony after testimony of our needs being met, of moving in ministry and jobs, and of healing and finances, because God has given me His Word and I have believed it and applied it to our situations. Overcoming isn't an absence of problems; it's the presence of the Word of God and His resurrection power.

My husband and I have both had cancer, and we are cancer free; Jim twelve years and me six years at the time of this writing. My husband has died three times, been in critical care for weeks, has had quintuple (five) bypass grafts to his heart, is on his second renal transplant, and he has had back surgery and arterial stents. I know what it's like to sit in ICU fighting fear and death while looking at machines and reports. I know the victory that comes in the night when God's Word becomes alive inside me and fires up mountain-moving faith to produce the miraculous.

I wrote this book from thirty-seven years of walking with God and seeing Him perform His Word. I have worked in medicine, taken overseas medical missions trips to bring healing, and taught medical students. I have a deep desire to heal the sick and show them Jesus. Jim and I are here today as living witnesses that God wants His creation well. God is faithful. Healing is real; our part is to believe God and submit to Him. God is a good God, full of love and mercy. He wants us well more than we want to be well. Trust Him, begin to pray for the sick, and expect Him to perform His Word. This is my prayer for you:

Father, I pray for the one reading this book, that You give them Your wisdom and understanding. That You teach them how to walk by faith and fulfill Your call on their life. I pray for the one reading this book that is sick and needs a miracle, that You will give them life and healing. I pray for the one reading this book who wants to be born again, that You will make them a new creation in Christ.

You have created us to rule and reign on this earth and have sent Your Son so that in Him we may accomplish Your will for our lives. We desire to see the lost saved, the sick healed, and the broken made whole, so that You might be glorified. That You fill up what is missing. That Your voice will be clear to them and that their desire to heal the sick will be realized. As You manifest in their lives for the good of others, let them be careful to stay humble and give You all the glory for what only You can do through them. Thank You, Father, for sending the Holy Spirit to teach them. Lead them in the paths You have chosen and into the good works You prepared long ago. In Jesus's name. Amen.

Questions

1. What does our tongue have the power to do?_____
_____

2. Why is it important to watch our words?_____
_____
_____

3. What is faith? _____
_____

4. What goes forth when we speak God's Word? _____
_____

5. How does lifestyle help us stay healed?_____
_____
_____

6. List some of the ways the devil deceives a person._____
_____
_____

7. What do I do if the symptoms return? _____
_____
_____

8. Why do symptoms return?_____
_____

9. Why do we need fresh revelation of God's Word?_____
_____
_____

10. Why does God want me well? _____
_____
_____

Reflections: _____

_____

_____

_____

_____

_____

_____

_____

_____

_____

_____

_____

_____

Prayers: _____

_____

_____

_____

_____

_____

_____

_____

_____

_____

_____

_____

_____

Additional Scripture References for Study

Proverbs 24:3-4, Genesis 1:1-31, Hebrews 11:1, James 3:5-8, Romans 14:23, John 6:63, Isaiah 55:11, Deuteronomy 8:3, Matthew 4:4, Matthew 12:43-45

Suggested Book Resources

The Authority of the Believer by John MacMillan
Divine Healing by Andrew Murray
Flowing in the Holy Ghost by Rodney Howard-Browne
Healing the Sick by T. L. Osborn
I Believe in Miracles by Kathryn Kuhlman
More Power by Bill Juoni
Rules of Engagement by Derek Prince
Smith Wigglesworth: A Man Who Walked with God by George Stormont

About the Author

Born at MacDill AFB in Tampa, Florida, I grew up in the military, living in England and Orlando, Florida. Upon graduation I entered ORMC School of Radiologic Technology, graduating two years later. In 1981 I surrendered my life to Jesus, was born again, and received the baptism of the Holy Spirit. My medical career took on a new purpose when I began to pray with my patients. I saw Jesus touch them, comfort them, and heal them. I wanted people to miraculously get well and not suffer. Jesus was the answer to their every need. He could heal their hurts, forgive their sins, and give them eternal life.

I met and married Jim McIlvaine in 1990. He also worked in the fields of radiology and cardiology. In 1996 we responded to God's call on our life and began taking short-term medical missions trips to the nations of Ukraine and Honduras. God directed us to start a nonprofit charity in 2000. It is a 501c3 Christian medical organization called Life House Ministries.

From 1996 to 2007 we shipped twenty tons of medical and humanitarian aid to churches, physicians, and pastors in the nation of Ukraine. We took medical professionals with us annually for the purpose of evangelism and free medical care. We traveled and worked throughout Ukraine, helping local churches grow, preaching, and assisting in building churches. Our clinics were held inside churches while the pastor preached and prayed with every patient. For ten years we supported an orphanage, which housed 237 mentally handicapped children with birth defects from the radiation disaster at Chernobyl. We also sponsored a drug and alcohol rehabilitation center in Lugansk. Our time in Ukraine ended in 2014 as God closed the door and prepared us for the next phase.

I retired in 2012, following a successful forty-five-year medical career in patient care and education. For three years we battled through Jim's health issues and surgeries. My husband and I are trophies of God's grace. Jim has been through countless surgeries and procedures, beginning at birth. Jesus has seen him through every sickness and surgery. Jim is my biggest inspiration of faith, perseverance, and a man who believes and trusts God. He is a wonderful provider and has encouraged me to be more than I ever could have been. He is my husband and my best friend. Above all else, he is a faithful follower of Jesus Christ.

I wrote this book to give hope to those who are sick, to teach you how to believe God for healing, and to bring glory to Jesus Christ. Healing is real, faith in God does move mountains, and you can be healed of anything because nothing is too difficult or impossible for God.

Made in the USA
Lexington, KY
28 September 2018